Renaissance

Cross Stitch
Samplers

RENAISSANCE
CROSS STITCH SAMPLERS

Angela Wainwright

CASSELL

A CASSELL BOOK

First published 1995
by Cassell
Wellington House
125 Strand
London WC2R 0BB

Produced by Rosemary Wilkinson
4 Lonsdale Square
London N1 1EN

Distributed in the United States
by Sterling Publishing Co., Inc.
387 Park Avenue South, New York,
New York 10016-8810

Distributed in Australia
By Capricorn Link (Australia) Pty Ltd
2/13 Carrington Road
Castle Hill
NSW 2154

Design and chart artwork: Pentrix Design
Photography: Mark Gatehouse
Illustrations: Stephen Dew
Picture research: Jane Lewis
Sampler mounts: Delia Elliman
Colour reproduction: Tenon & Polert Ltd

British Library Cataloguing-in-Publication Data
A catalogue record for this book is available from the British Library

ISBN 0-304-34441-9 (hardback)
ISBN 0-304-34694-2 (paperback)

Printed and bound in Italy

Contents

Historical Background

The Renaissance was a period in European history of brilliant accomplishment, encompassing all areas of cultural life, which gathered pace from its beginnings in Italy in the 14th century, to its height in the 15th and 16th centuries and continuing elsewhere in Europe through to the mid-17th century. It was fuelled by a new humanitarian philosophy, which was based on the belief that man was in charge of his own destiny and no longer at the mercy of fate. This fresh perception on life brought about a self-confidence which manifested itself in the great explosion of accomplishment in literature, science, exploration and the arts, throughout the whole of Europe.

Essential to the development of Renaissance thinking, indeed it was the catalyst, was the rediscovery of classical books and manuscripts. Through the study of these works the classical ideals of the Greek and Roman empires were reintroduced. The invention of printing at the same time enabled the discoveries to be more readily available to a greater number of people for study and interpretation. The ideals and accompanying styles were sympathetically received and the Renaissance period was born.

Medieval art had been largely impersonal and anonymous. Renaissance man's growing confidence that he was of direct importance in the moulding of civilization led him to initial his creations, which was an important development for us, as we seek to attribute and date the surviving pieces.

The Italians were the first to incorporate classical architectural principles into their work and this inevitably was mirrored quite quickly by the absorption of a similar style into other areas of the decorative arts, such as literature, music and fine art.

In essence the Renaissance style of painting was an adaptation of the classical form, but using a freer line, particularly where floral motifs formed the central theme of the design, as they often did. The discovery of wall paintings during extensive excavation of ancient ruins showed much use of botanical forms and this was transmitted to the Renaissance style, so that everywhere the delicate, curved, often symmetrical stems, leaves and flowers of vine, ivy, fruit and particularly the ancient acanthus predominated. The human figure in natural form, and animals, realistically portrayed or fantastical in shape,

◆ A lithograph of a design by Bérain
c. 1670 for a marvellously ornate
tapestry.

were interlaced among this foliage and in the later part of the period, a variety of heraldic devices, such as cartouches (ornamental frames designed to enclose an inscription), further embellished the style. The 15th century saw the most rapid progress in this style of ornamental painting, though the seeds had been sewn for a more realistic representation of the human form as far back as the second half of the 13th century, by Giotto di Bondone.

Stained glass design was affected by a swing to the secular and, in England, by the dissolution of the monasteries. The glass painters' and artists' work moved from an emphasis on the ornamentation of religious buildings and relevant subject matter, to civic and private building decoration, producing the more realistic style, often historical and symbolical or heraldic in content. These were more fitting subjects for the private house or for the many new universities and colleges that sprang up and flourished throughout Europe with the increase in the quest for knowledge by the layman at this time.

Domestic life, at least for the wealthy, underwent great changes. Houses were built no longer with the primary aim of providing a fortified building, but with comfort as the main requirement and the overall desire to create a grand home. In England in the 16th century the Tudor Gothic style (a simplification of the grand Renaissance style) evolved, featuring flattened arches, towers, ornate chimneys and square mullioned windows which let plenty of light into the house.

Inside the house there was also an increase in decoration, first with insulating wall-hangings, then by the 16th century, with wall carpets, followed by silk and linen tapestry hangings. The popularity and success of this among the wealthy led to the development of the famous Gobelin tapestry workshop in France, during the reign of Louis XIV.

A number of projects within this book are based on French faience work. 'Faience' is the name given to 17th century earthenware pottery, which followed the principles of the earlier 'majolica' style, which was lustre glazed, beautifully decorated and highly coloured ware of Hispano-Moorish origin. The earlier 'majolica' ware imported originally via Majorca (hence its name) became extremely popular and the demand for it eventually led to the establishment of workshops in parts of Italy, where the style was reproduced. The potters of one such workshop in Faenza introduced their craft into France, the Low Countries and Spain and this led to later dated pieces being referred to as 'faience' work. The craft flourished in France, in particular, under the direction of Hougest and Gouffier, whose designs were exceptionally delicate.

Costumes and textiles were also influenced by the Renaissance style. The rich silks and velvets used were heavily embroidered with floral and geometric styles, exquisite Italian lace work adorned cuffs and collars and fine lawn chemises were delicately embroidered with blackwork motifs. Skill with the needle became a crucial asset and this fashion for embellishment helps to explain the emergence at this time of the practice sampler as embroiderers constantly sought to improve their skills and to widen their range of patterns.

The increased movement of people across Europe led to many foreign artists and craftsmen settling in England. Among such men was the thirty-year-old Hans Holbein, whose royal patronage has left us with a wonderful legacy of court portraiture to add to our knowledge and understanding of Renaissance style in costume.

The designs for table carpets, bed hangings, etc, were often taken from popular engravings and paintings, many fine examples of which have survived to this day. They are worked in tent stitch on a fine linen canvas showing scenes from rural life (the Elizabethan ideal) and they, in their turn, can prove a valuable source of pattern for our needlework projects today. Canvas work gained a popularity during the 16th century, imitating the beautiful, but to most, unaffordable, tapestries hung in the great houses. Like the table carpets, scenes were essentially rural, with animals and flowers providing a carpet of motifs among which scenes of biblical or mythical stories featured.

During the 15th century, because the demand for decoration was so great, workshops were established where individual designs, intended for the new fashion of single motif adornment, were produced and kept until they were needed for a particular item; mass production in its infancy! Orders would be gained for these motifs through representatives of the workshop, rather than craftsmen awaiting commissions before commencing work.

A by-product of the new printing developments was the greater availability of pattern books to the needlewomen. Unfortunately, very few of these have survived as the patterns were often used directly onto the fabrics; the designs being transferred by pricking and punching onto the fabric. The patterns contained within these books were often for borders intended to be worked on household linen and clothing. The first squared paper designs were also printed in black and white, intended for counted thread embroidery, or for lacis, a form of darning on hand-knotted square net mesh.

English domestic embroidery skills during the second half of the 16th century were unsurpassed. Since all ecclesiastical embroidery halted with the Reformation, the skills were transferred to the embellishment of home textiles. The gentle ladies and noblewomen who would have concerned themselves with church vestments and altar cloths now had a chance to use their time for the beautification of themselves, their families and their homes using the rich silks, silver and gold thread they would have saved for their former work.

'Blackwork' earlier confined to cuffs, collars and general edging, now developed and expanded into 'all over' patterns embroidered in double running stitch. Worked in both geometric and floral shapes, it coiled across sleeves, providing a sharp contrast to the richly coloured and denser embroidery to be found on the brocades and velvets.

Scrollwork and abstract geometrics were particularly popular on the continent while the late 16th century needlewomen in England chose less formal, more crowded floral and animal motifs, basing their ideas upon the many herbals available. 'Slips' were worked (see page 36) and applied to domestic linen. Counted thread embroidery gained in popularity for use on small personal items as well as for larger projects.

The starched collars worn by members of the court in the late 16th century provided a splendid showpiece for open work effects and whitework techniques were as a consequence expanded. The fineness of Italian cutwork in particular was exquisite.

◆ A pair of intricately embroidered early 17th century gloves and an initialled handkerchief, both trimmed with exquisite lace work.

There is no doubt that samplers in some form were in existence before the late 15th century but they were practice or reference pieces kept in a workbox and therefore with no care taken to preserve them. The earliest dated sampler that has come to light, and attributed to Jane Bostocke (1598), is a forerunner of the personalization that became standard during the 17th century. The spot samplers (discussed later in the book) provided small motif ideas for small items, such as purses, book covers and frames, and this use, rather than their application to practical domestic items, gained in popularity during the 17th century. Band samplers (again, discussed later in the book) continued to have a more practical function but by the mid-17th century they began to undergo a subtle change, from an essential reference piece for stitches and patterns towards a complete piece of work designed to be displayed.

Human figures began to appear and little creatures, such as caterpillars, butterflies and snails joined the larger bird and animal motifs. The principle of practising dexterity with the needle was still the main aim of sampler work but this was increasingly combined with the desire to produce a display piece.

Undertaken for a purpose and fulfilling a need, the embroidery of the period was a craft equal in importance to all the other decorative and applied arts during this time of unequalled creative activity.

It is not possible to give a definitive appraisal of the period in such a short chapter. However, I have tried to give an insight into the overall picture, to provide you, the stitcher, with a little background knowledge which you may find interesting and may like to muse upon as you stitch pieces for the future.

MATERIALS

1 piece of white Belfast linen, 32 count,
19 x 22 in (47 x 54 cm)

tapestry needle(s) size 26

lightweight wadding for mounting (optional)

1 skein each of stranded cotton in the
following shades:

		DMC	Anchor
	moss green	3346	267
	pale moss green	3348	264
	pale green	368	214
	pale navy	312	979
	brick red	3328	10
	pale brick red	760	9
	new gold	3820	306

3 skeins of stranded cotton in:

	green-gold	833	907
	dusty blue	334	977
	dark antique blue	3750	123
	v. dark brown-pink	221	897

Finished size of design: 12⅖ x 15⅖ in
(31.5 x 39 cm)

Tudor Spot Sampler

A colourful, undated, but thought to be mid-17th century, spot sampler worked in silks, silver and silver gilt threads gives us the lattice frame-work for this project. The original, which is housed at the Victoria & Albert Museum in London, is worked on linen.

The 'spot' or 'random' sampler is so-called from the fact that patterns and motifs were 'spotted' indiscriminately on strips of linen. This and the placing of patterns in strips or bands are the two characteristics of traditional samplers of this period. The sampler itself was a way by which needlewomen kept a reference library of stitches and patterns used, or for future use, on their personal or domestic embroidered items.

The economical use of every possible space on these samplers (fabric and silk were very expensive) has added to their charm; the needle-women creating for us, their descendants, a marvellous diversity of shapes and colours and an encyclopedia of motifs that we can continue to use to this day.

Flowers with symbolic meanings, domestic animals, exotic and fantastical creatures, geometric shapes and lattice work patterns, such as the stylized Tudor rose used in this project, all feature strongly in the surviving examples. All kinds of stitches were used: Florentine, cross, rice, double running and Algerian eye, to name but a few.

◆ Right: This is a classic spot sampler in which the 17th century embroiderer has recorded all kinds of motifs from a mermaid to a thistle, including a short section of a lattice which has given the basic structure to the Tudor Spot Sampler (far right).

The geometric design forming the overlay at the top of the project is derived from a carpet border on an Italian picture. Full length portraits of royalty or the wealthy painted during this period often show the subject standing upon a richly patterned carpet, with geometric designs featuring strongly. By the mid-16th century carpets had begun to replace rushes as floor covering for those who could afford them and their inclusion in the portraits is often a statement of the subject's wealth and standing. Taken from ancient designs and mostly Italian in origin, the carpets featured in the paintings provide us with a wealth of designs suitable for cross stitch work. Do take time to study them.

The internal or diaper patterns are adapted from spot motifs found on a sampler held at the Victoria & Albert Museum and the blackwork

◆ Part of a mid-17th century band sampler which has a charming selection of blackwork motifs of all kinds filling all the available space at the top followed by some complex floral bands, one of which has been used for the Pattern Band Sampler later in the book

motifs (i.e. those worked in a double running stitch) are derived from two mid-17th century samplers, one at the Victoria & Albert Museum, the other at the Fitzwilliam Museum, Cambridge.

METHOD

As this is quite a detailed project that will take some time to complete, I strongly recommend that you hem or tack the raw edges of the fabric before starting to cross stitch, to prevent fraying (see page 90).

Fold the fabric in half lengthwise to find the centre vertical line and crease lightly. Now measure down this fold for 3 in (7.5 cm) from the top of the fabric. This will give the point at which you start stitching. Find the starting stitch marked on the chart on page 19 and begin work on the fabric with this stitch.

Use two strands of cotton, working over two thread intersections. Work the outlines in back stitch and the rest in cross stitch.

From the starting stitch work approximately twenty stitches either to the left or to the right, then work the pattern below these for about twenty rows. Return to the starting stitch and work in the opposite direction, thus allowing the design to build up in blocks. This should prevent calculation mistakes, which are so easy to make when counting straight lines of stitches! Continue in this way, leaving any back stitch outlining until you have completed all the other parts of the design. Finally add your initials using the alphabet from the Band Pattern Sampler (page 33) and planning the letter spacing as described on page 92.

When the stitching is complete, wash if necessary and press gently from the wrong side (see page 90). For finishing and mounting instructions, see page 92.

◆ A highly colourful spot sampler with both marvellously natural interpretations of plants and animals and more stylized plants and geometric patterns.

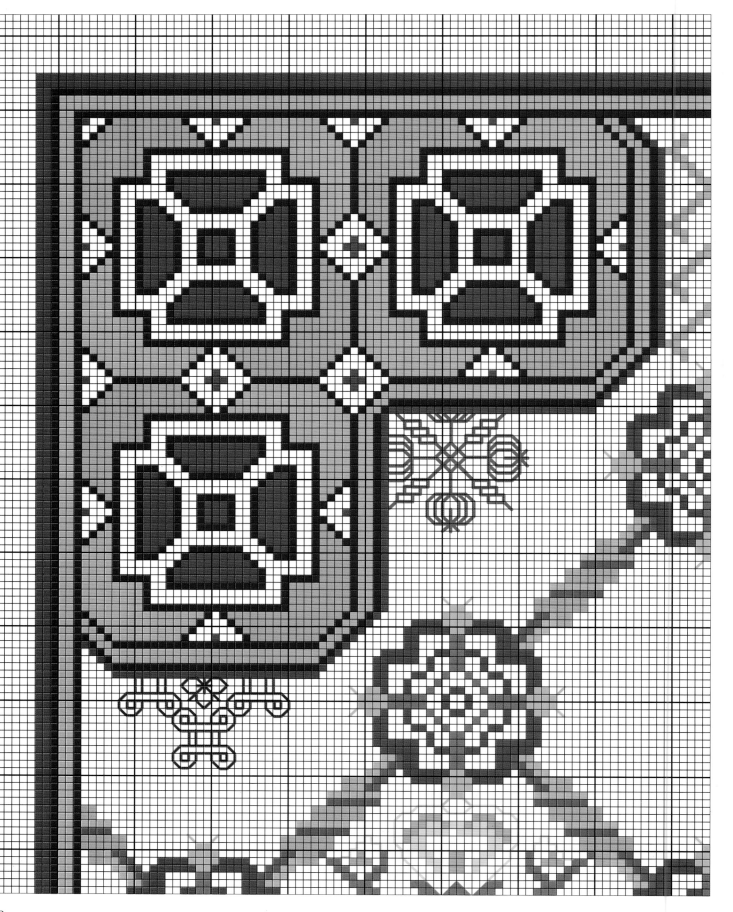

18

19

MATERIALS

4 pieces of white Aida, 14 count, each 3 x 3 in (7.5 x 7.5 cm)

1 piece of white Aida, 18 count, 4 x 4 in (10 x 10 cm)

5 pieces of iron-on interfacing, same size as Aida

tapestry needle, size 24

4 gift tag blanks with circular apertures (see page 93 for stockist)

1 card mount with 3 in (7.5 cm) diameter aperture (see page 93 for stockist)

fabric adhesive

1 skein each of stranded cotton in the following shades:

		DMC	Anchor
▰	*dark green*	319	217
▰	*red*	666	46

Finished size of designs:

a) 1½ x 1½ in (4 x 4 cm)

b) 1⅛ x 1⅛ in (3 x 3 cm)

c) ¾ x ¾ in (2 x 2 cm)

d) ¾ x ¾ in (2 x 2 cm)

e) ¾ x 1 in (2 x 2.5 cm)

Gift Stationery

The designs for the large samplers in this book are created from a variety of period sources, which present a fund of ready-made motifs for smaller projects. These Christmas gift tags are an example of this secondary usage. The designs make use of the blackwork motifs from the English band sampler of the mid-17th century shown on page 16, originally sourced for the Tudor Spot Sampler.

Stitched cards are also an ideal way of using up any oddments of fabric and threads you may have accumulated from previous work.

METHOD

Work as follows for all five designs.

Fold the fabric in half lengthwise and crosswise to find the centre point. Crease lightly. Begin work at this point following the starting stitch marked on the relevant chart below.

Work in cross stitch and back stitch using three strands of cotton over one thread intersection for the 14 count Aida and two strands over one intersection for the 18 count.

When the stitching is complete, place the interfacing centrally on the reverse of the work and iron in position. Trim and mount in the cards following the instructions on page 92.

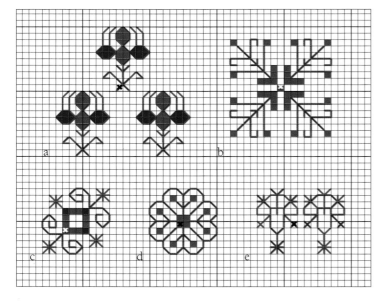

◆ Right: Quick and easy to work for a busy time of year, these little designs could easily be worked in alternative shades for gifts on other special occasions.

Two Botanical Pictures

These two floral motifs have been taken from the 17th century sampler on page 17 which also provided the design inspiration for the Tudor Spot Sampler (page 15). The carnation and pomegranate were popular and symbolic motifs used in embroidery at this period to embellish both clothing and domestic items.

The pomegranate symbolized the Hope of Eternal Life and when worked with an open seed pod, represented the spread of Christian

teaching. It was also a royal emblem during the late 16th century. Catherine of Aragon, Henry VIII's first wife, and their daughter, Mary, adopted it as one of their badges. Worked mostly as a spot motif, it can also be found in more stylized form as a repeat border.

Religious symbolism is also attached to the carnation. Indeed, most of the flowers used on 16th and 17th embroidery had religious connotations. The origins of the meaning attributed to this flower extend way back before the Renaissance period, in that it was the Flower of Zeus, but by the 16th century it had come to represent, like the rose, the Flower of Heavenly Bliss and if shown in paintings or stained glass with

◆ **Above: The addition of the same border pattern adapted from an enamelled copper motif (top) is an effective way of making a set out of different flower and fruit designs.**

MATERIALS

To work both designs:

2 pieces of cream Belfast linen, 32 count, each 19 x 19 in (49 x 49 cm)

tapestry needle(s), size 26

lightweight wadding for mounting (optional)

1 skein each of stranded cotton in the following shades:

		DMC	Anchor
carnation			
	very pale green	369	213
	moss green	3346	267
	pale moss green	3348	264
	brick red	3328	10
	pale brick red	760	9
	v. pale brick red	761	23
	palest brick red	3713	968
pomegranate			
	darkest khaki	936	846
	khaki	470	266
	very pale khaki	472	278
	new pale gold	3822	305
	coffee	3045	888
	light coffee	3046	887
	pale coffee	3047	886
	white	blanc	1
border (both designs)			
	gold	783	307
	dark bronze	730	924
	light bronze	733	280
	pine green	580	924
	pale petrol blue	519	167

2 skeins of stranded cotton in:

	pale bronze	734	279

Finished size of both designs: 11 ³/₄ x 11 ³/₄ in (29.5 x 29.5 cm)

the Virgin Mary, Divine Love. Like the pomegranate, it was commonly worked as a single motif but also widely used in a variety of stylized forms as a repeat border.

The border pattern surrounding these two flowers is derived from motifs on ornaments enamelled in copper, in the early Limoges, champlevé style (the enamel was fired in depressions made in the metal) and from Limoges painted enamels, all of the 16th century. These may be found in the Hotel Cluny in Paris. The same pattern is used on both to make a matching pair of pictures but the flowers could be stitched successfully without the border.

METHOD

Work as follows for both pictures.

As for the samplers, I recommend that you hem or tack the raw edges of the fabric before starting to cross stitch, in order to prevent fraying (see page 90).

Fold the fabric in half lengthwise and crosswise, then mark these lines with tacking stitches. This will mark the centre point at which you start stitching on the fabric. Find the starting stitch marked on the relevant chart on page 25 or 26 and begin work on the fabric with this stitch.

Work in cross stitch and back stitch using two strands of cotton over two thread intersections. Stitch the central flower first, then the border. To work the pomegranate border, measure 4 ¹/₄ in (11 cm) from the starting stitch up the centre vertical line of tacking. This positions the centre stitch of the bottom line of the border. Follow the chart on page 25 to work the border.

When the stitching is complete, wash if necessary and press gently from the wrong side (see page 90). For finishing and mounting instructions, see page 92.

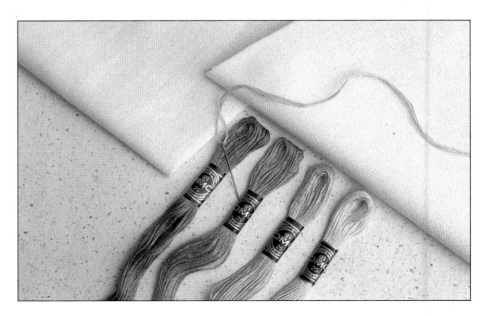

MATERIALS

Teapot Stand

1 piece of white Aida, 16 count, 9 x 9 in (23 x 23 cm)

1 teapot stand (see page 93 for stockist)

1 piece of iron-on interfacing, same size as Aida

1 skein each of stranded cotton in the following shades:

		DMC	Anchor
■	black	310	403
■	red-brown	355	341
■	medium brown	3772	914
■	very dark brown	3371	382
■	dark khaki	469	267
■	pale khaki	471	265
□	v. pale khaki	472	278
■	pale navy	312	979

Finished size of design: 3 1/3 x 2 2/3 in (8.5 x 7 cm)

◆ **Far right: The bright and cheerful colours of the parrot have kept their appeal through the ages from the 17th century to the present day.**

Teapot Stand

This design takes another motif from the same spot sampler as the previous two pictures. The cheeky parrot, displayed here in a useful teapot stand, could alternatively be incorporated into a special sampler for a child. The parrot was an extremely popular motif with the Victorians and it is interesting to see its use much earlier in a mid 17th century sampler (see page 17).

Both real and imaginary animals and birds feature strongly in spot sampler work. Although useful and pretty in a purely decorative sense, the inclusion of stylized forms was probably done as practice for heraldic use; not just for formal badges but for use on the livery of the retainers and the embellishment of the furnishings and personal items of wealthy or titled families.

METHOD

Fold the fabric in half lengthwise and crosswise to find the centre point. Crease lightly. Start work at this point following the stitch marked on the chart opposite.

Work in cross stitch using two strands of cotton over one thread intersection.

When the stitching is complete, wash if necessary and press gently from the wrong side (see page 90). Place the interfacing centrally on the reverse of the work and iron in position. Trim and place the fabric centrally in the mount following the manufacturer's instructions.

Cushion Cover

The 17th century sampler used for the previous three designs and illustrated on page 17 also provides the grape and vine motif for this cushion cover. This was a classic design motif of the period due to its religious symbolism and biblical connotations and therefore much used on church vestments. It is often presented, as here, as a large bunch of grapes with a single vine leaf and curling tendrils. It is used in a more abstract version on page 63.

I have shown possible uses for several of the spot motifs from this marvellous sampler but there are plenty more for you to adapt for your own designs.

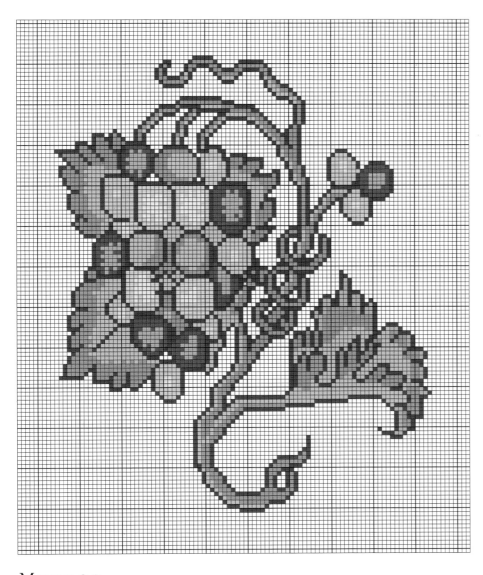

MATERIALS

To make a 12 in (30 cm) cushion

2 pieces of ivory or cream Linda, 27 count, each 14 x 14 in (35 x 35 cm) or 1 piece of Linda and 1 piece of backing fabric of your own choice

tapestry needle, size 24

braid, 50 in (125 cm) long (optional)

1 cushion pad, 12 in (30 cm) square

sewing cotton in shade of fabric

1 skein each of stranded cotton in the following shades:

		DMC	Anchor
	pale navy	312	979
	dusty blue	334	977
	khaki	470	266
	pale khaki	471	265
	v. pale khaki	472	278
	olive green	936	846
	pale brick red	760	9
	v. pale brick red	761	23
	pale mushroom	950	4146
	light mushroom	3774	778

Finished size of design: 7 x 8⅞ in (18 x 22.5 cm)

METHOD

First tack or oversew the edges of the fabric to prevent fraying (see page 90), then fold the Aida in half lengthwise and crosswise to find the centre point. Crease lightly. Start work at this point following the stitch marked on the chart above.

Work in cross stitch using two strands of cotton over two thread intersections to give a denser look to the stitching.

When the stitching is complete, remove tacking and press gently from the wrong side. Place the embroidery and the fabric for the back with right sides together. Pin and machine stitch or back stitch by hand round the edges, making a 1 in (2.5 cm) seam and leaving part of one side open. Trim the seam to ½ in (13 mm) and across the corners. Turn right side out. Insert the cushion pad into the cover, then turn under the remaining raw edges and slip stitch the opening together. Slip stitch the braid, if used, round the edges covering the seam lines.

◆ Left: The popular bunch of grapes motif makes an extremely attractive cushion cover but could also be stitched as a picture to match those on page 23.

Band Pattern Sampler

Popular during the 17th century, the traditional band sampler was worked in silks, silver and gold threads, embellished with beads and seed pearls and consisted of tightly packed lines of repeat patterns, geometric and stylized floral in content. Sometimes spot motifs were used in conjunction with the band work and as on the spot samplers, a great number of stitches were used, since band samplers were produced with the same purpose in mind: that of practising and cataloguing designs.

Floral patterns were the most common and the most frequently stitched flowers were the carnation, the honeysuckle and the rose. Strawberry, pansy and acorn motifs were also popular. The reason for the constant use of these particular flower heads, apart from the simple beauty of their shape, was the symbolism attached to them.

The rose has held symbolic significance for centuries. As a pagan symbol it signified Earthly Love; to the Romans, Pride and Victory and to subsequent generations, a mixture of all of these as well as being a symbol of Divine Love when it was shown with the Virgin. The Honeysuckle symbolizes Enduring Faith and was a favourite flower at the time, believed by some to hold the power to fend off the evil eye. The violet represented Humility, and the carnation, like the rose, Divine Love. The trefoil shape of the pansy is a traditional symbol of the Holy Trinity and the purple and yellow variety was a particular favourite of Elizabeth I, adding to its popularity.

The designs in this Band Sampler are drawn from a variety of sources representative of the decorative and applied arts of the Renaissance. Sources for the bands, some of which are illustrated, are as follows:

- Birds from Frances Bridon's sampler, housed at the Fitzwilliam Museum, Cambridge.
- A section of marble mosaic from the Museo Pio Clementino in Rome.
- Blackwork from a band sampler held in the Fitzwilliam Museum.
- Honeysuckle pattern as found on a sampler held in the Victoria & Albert Museum, London.
- Bas-relief fretwork from Genoa.
- Quatrefoil ornamentation from a building dating around 1660.
- Stone sculpture work from the Château du Blois (1530).
- Embroidered European linen.
- A traditionally shaped alphabet as found on many samplers.

The project could be worked exactly as shown, or the individual repeat patterns could be worked as borders on further sampler work. If you choose to do this and wish to take the design round a corner, take a hand mirror and hold it vertically against the sampler design at a 45° angle across the chosen border. The reflection will give the corner repeat.

This design is also a rich source of motifs for other projects. The little bib which follows gives just one suggestion.

◆ **Above: A selection of Renaissance designs from a variety of different art forms originally, all translated here into cross stitch patterns.**
Right: Our band sampler is a record of some of the most common Renaissance patterns taken from designs on buildings and textiles of the period.

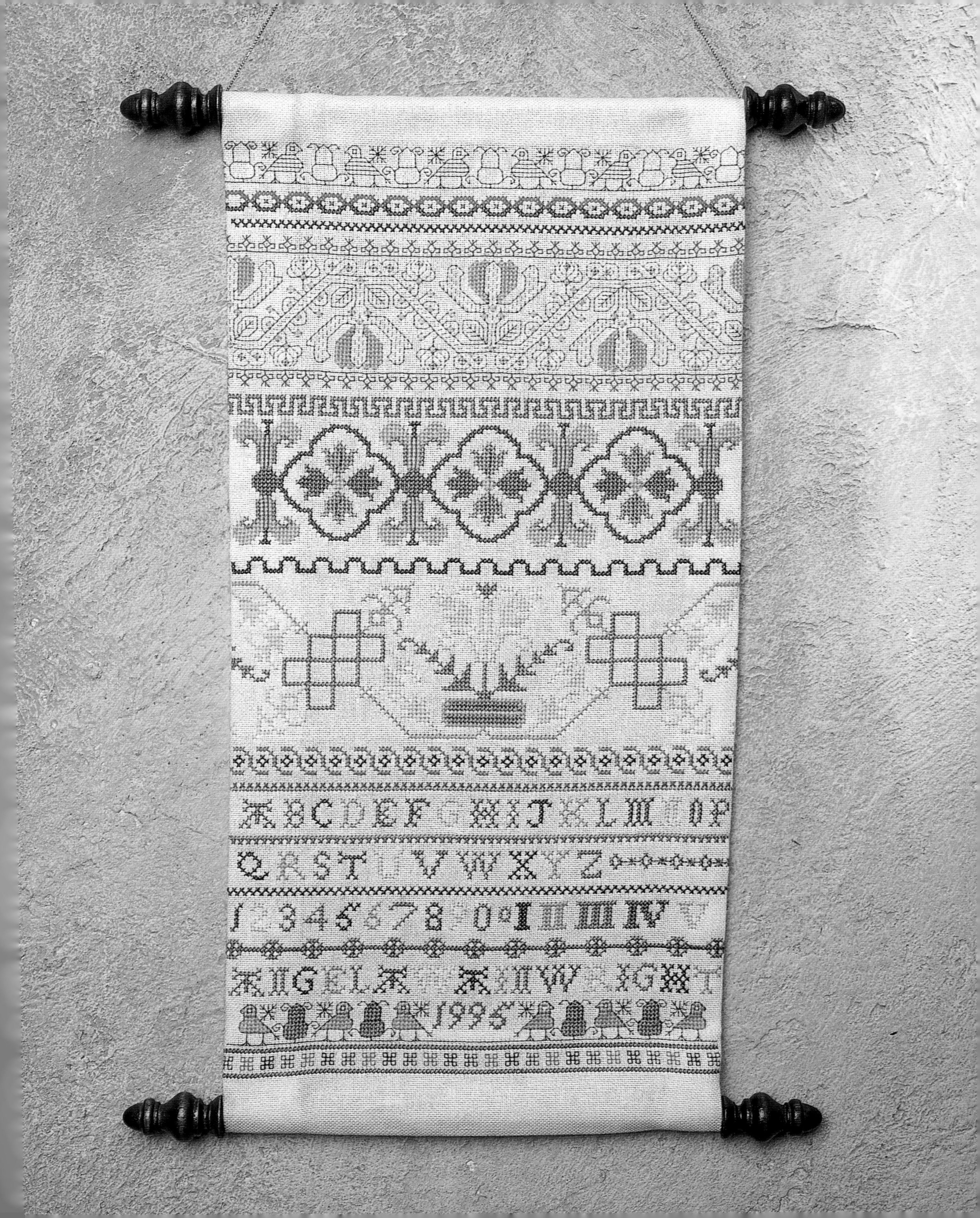
1996

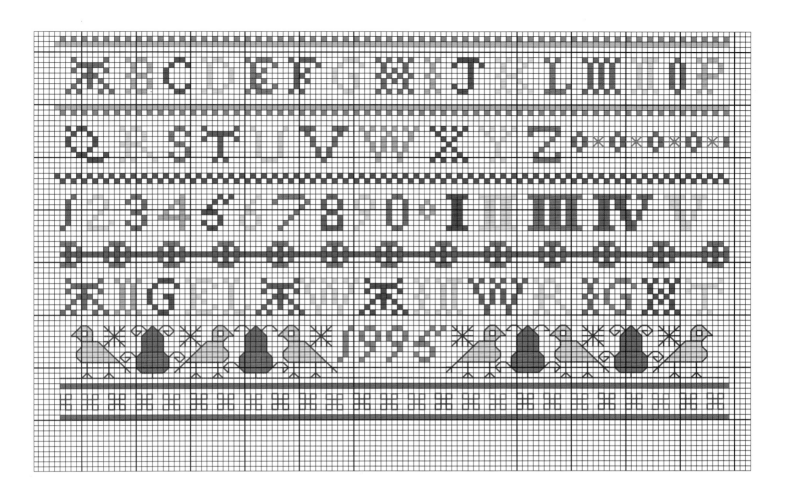

MATERIALS

*1 piece of cream Belfast linen, 32 count,
12 x 24 in (30 x 60 cm)*

tapestry needle(s), size 26

1 pair bell pull ends, 7 in (18 cm) wide

*1 skein each of stranded cotton in the
following shades:*

		DMC	Anchor
	medium red-brown	356	5975
	orange-brown	919	340
	pale brick red	760	9
	light grey	414	235
	pale gold	726	295
	dark green-gold	832	907
	light blue	799	145
	antique mauve	3041	871
	dark moss green	3345	268
	light moss green	3347	266
	pale moss green	3348	264
	new red	3801	335
	new blue	3807	122
	new light brown	3827	362

*Finished size of design: 8⅞ x 16½ in
(22.5 x 42.5 cm)*

METHOD

Fold the fabric in half lengthwise to find the centre vertical line. Crease lightly. Measure 4 in (10 cm) down this line from the top of the fabric and begin stitching at this point following the starting point marked on the chart on page 32.

As this is a heavily worked sampler, I recommend that you tack or oversew the edges to prevent fraying (see page 90), but do this after you have established the starting stitch, otherwise the measurements will not be accurate.

Work in cross stitch and back stitch using two strands of cotton over two thread intersections.

From the starting stitch, work either to the right or to the left stitching the line of birds and acorns. Return to the centre and complete the band by working in the opposite direction. Continue to work in this way, band by band, to the bottom of the sampler, although having initially established the centre of the design, you may start stitching from either the left or the right of the design for subsequent bands.

Lastly, add your own name to the base of the sampler using letters from the alphabet you have just stitched and following the instructions on letter spacing given on page 92.

When the stitching is complete, wash if necessary and press gently from the wrong side (see page 90). Hem the two long sides of the sampler, using a ½ in (13 mm) hem allowance, then turn a hem at top and bottom deep enough to allow the bell pull ends to be inserted.

◆ **Above: Part of a beautifully stitched
sampler by a ten-year-old girl practising her letters and her needlework at
the same time gives the first and last
patterns on the band sampler.**

Baby Bib

This useful bib uses the pretty bird motifs from Frances Bridon's sampler which also appear on the Band Pattern Sampler (see page 34). The birds are worked in back stitch filled in with cross stitch. Originally such motifs were either left unfilled or filled with satin stitch.

The bib is shown worked in shades of peach for a little girl but an alternative colourway for a boy is given in the list of shades. The name of the child could be added above the pattern if liked, following the instructions for letter spacing given on page 92. The pattern would also look very effective worked on a towel to form a baby set.

MATERIALS

1 bib with evenweave band
tapestry needle, size 24
1 skein each of stranded cotton in the following shades:

		DMC	Anchor
for a girl:			
■	*pale grey*	*318*	*399*
▨	*peach*	*352*	*9*
▨	*pale peach*	*353*	*6*
▨	*dark green-gold*	*832*	*907*
▨	*pale moss green*	*3348*	*264*
for a boy:			
■	*pale grey*	*318*	*399*
▨	*blue*	*798*	*131*
▨	*very pale blue*	*800*	*144*
▨	*dark green-gold*	*832*	*907*
▨	*pale moss green*	*3348*	*264*

Finished size of pattern shown: 6 x ¾ in (15.5 x 2 cm)

METHOD

Fold the bib in half lengthwise to find the centre horizontal line of the band and crease lightly. Find the centre point of the depth of the band by counting the holes in the evenweave fabric. Start work at this point following the starting stitch marked on the chart below. Stitch one complete motif, then continue stitching motifs on either side as required.

Using two strands of cotton over one thread intersection, work in cross stitch first, then complete the outlines in back stitch.

◆ **Left: The naïve bird and acorn pattern works perfectly on a baby's bib.**

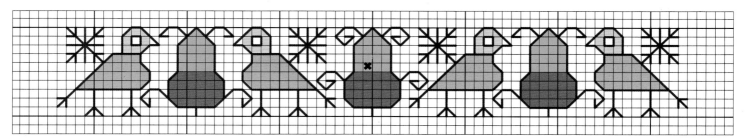

Honeysuckle Sampler

The motif for this project is adapted from a 'slip' found on a 17th century velvet bed hanging, featuring a central heraldic device and held at Hardwick Hall, Derbyshire (see page 40).

The term 'slip' applies to an embroidery technique in which the motif is worked, usually in tent stitch, onto canvas. It is then cut out and appliquéed to the background fabric. The perimeter is overlaid with a thick silk thread which is couched down, then additional stitching is worked over the edges, extending onto the base fabric to hide any joins.

This method was used predominately for domestic articles. Clothes would often have the same patterns decorating them but these would be embroidered directly onto the fabric rather than applied.

The honeysuckle plant, for reasons explained in the Band Pattern Sampler project (page 30), was a favourite flower of the Renaissance period, often sourced at that time from the ever-growing number of herbals available. If you are lucky enough to have a honeysuckle growing in your garden, or better still if you live in a rural area where it grows wild, you will know how exquisite is the scent emanating from the plant at dusk and understand why it was so popular even without its strong religious significance.

This sampler could commemorate a variety of special occasions or it could be used as a pretty border for a passage of verse or a favourite saying. Table linen is another alternative use for the border.

Use the alphabet from the Band Pattern Sampler chart (page 33) to personalize your work or work from a backstitch alphabet if you intend stitching a longer verse, with perhaps a capital letter at the beginning of each line or verse.

◆ **Far right: Inspired by a motif on an antique bed hanging, the honeysuckle tendrils make a highly decorative border for a special message.**

MATERIALS

*1 piece of white or cream Aida, 16 count,
14 x 22 in (35.5 x 56 cm)*

tapestry needle, size 26

lightweight wadding for mounting (optional)

*1 skein each of stranded cotton in the
following shades:*

	DMC	Anchor
green	367	216
dark moss green	3345	268
v. pale gold	727	293
dark fawn	729	890
dark dusky pink	3350	65
light dusty rose	3733	75

2 skeins of stranded cotton in:

	DMC	Anchor
pale green	368	214

*Finished size of design: 7½ x 14½ in
(19 x 37 cm)*

◆ **Above: These richly embroidered bed
hangings adorn the State Bedroom at
Hardwick Hall in Derbyshire,
England.**
**Far right: The honeysuckle motif also
looks very attractive when worked on
a smaller scale.**

METHOD

Fold the fabric in half with shorter sides together to find the centre vertical line. Crease lightly. Measure 3 ½ in (9 cm) down this line from the top and commence stitching at this point following the starting stitch shown on the chart on page 38.

Work in cross stitch and back stitch using two strands of cotton over one thread intersection.

Stitch the design either to the left or the right of the starting point and complete the flowers on this side before going back to the centre and stitching the remaining half of the design. Although this may mean threading and unthreading needles more frequently than if you were completing each shade in turn, it will ensure that you position the motifs symmetrically. Complete the top line of motifs before working the side motifs and lastly the lower line.

Add your own personal details following the instructions on letter spacing given on page 92. When the stitching is complete, wash if necessary and press gently from the wrong side (see page 90). For finishing and mounting instructions, see page 92.

Dressing Table Set

A single honeysuckle motif taken from the large sampler on page 37 forms the design for this dressing table set, which would make a lovely complementary set to the sampler either for personal use or as a gift.

METHOD

Work as follows for both pieces.

Fold the fabric in half lengthwise and crosswise to find the centre point. Crease lightly. Begin work at this point following the starting stitch marked on the chart opposite.

Work in cross stitch using one strand of cotton over one thread intersection for the 22 count Aida and two strands over one intersection for the 18 count. Work the back stitch using one strand on both counts.

When the stitching is complete, press the fabric gently from the wrong side. Place the interfacing centrally on the reverse of the work and iron in position. Trim carefully to fit the mounts and assemble according to the manufacturer's instructions.

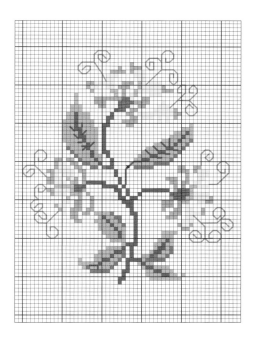

MATERIALS

1 piece of cream or white Aida, 18 count, 7 x 7 in (18 x 18 cm), for the mirror

1 piece of cream or white Aida, 22 count, 5 x 6 in (12.5 x 15 cm), for the hairbrush

tapestry needle, size 26

1 dressing table set (see page 93 for stockist)

2 pieces of iron-on interfacing, same size as Aida

1 skein each of stranded cotton in the following shades:

		DMC	Anchor
	green	367	216
	pale green	368	214
	v. pale gold	727	293
	dark fawn	729	890
	dark moss green	3345	268
	dark dusky pink	3350	65
	light dusty rose	3733	75

Finished size of design (mirror): 3 x 3¼ in (7.5 x 8.5 cm)

Finished size of design (hairbrush): 2⅜ x 2⅞ in (6 x 7.5 cm)

Marriage Sampler

The border for this project is based on French workmanship on a wooden cabinet made during the reign of James I. The focus of the design of newly built, larger houses during this period moved away from the need to fortify the building to more aesthetic considerations, with the result that more decorative features were introduced. Understandably, this greater attention to external ornamentation was mirrored internally in room design and from thence to domestic furnishings and furniture. Wood was used extensively as panelling and, in the grander houses, was heavily carved, reaching a height of complexity in early Jacobean times.

The corner motifs are devised from ornamental enamelling on copper in the Limoges champlevé style (see page 24) and housed in the Hotel Cluny, Paris.

The church is taken from a sampler of Dutch origin, now housed at the Zaanland Museum of Antiquities at Zaandijk. Church buildings and ecclesiastical objects begin to appear on Dutch samplers at this time

◆ **Above:** A typical Renaissance design for carved wood showing symmetrically intertwined plant forms gives the sampler border.
Right: An antique Dutch sampler provides the symbolic church motif.
Far right: This sampler combines decoration and symbols in commemoration of a special occasion.

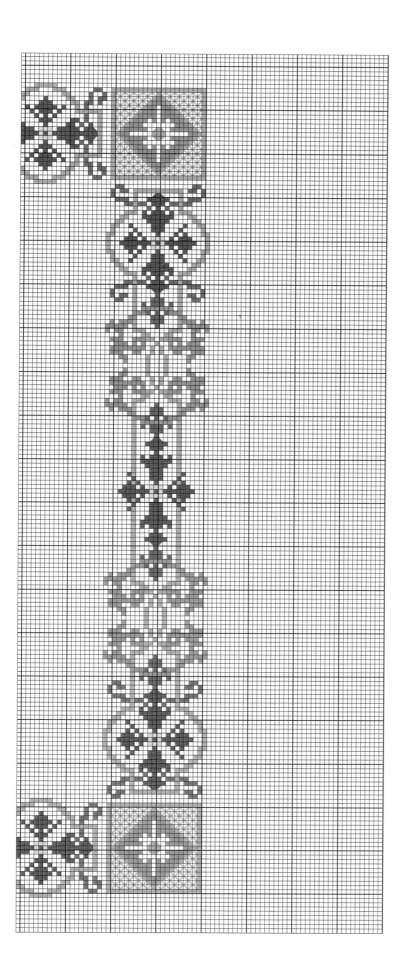

MATERIALS

*1 piece of cream Aida, 16 count, 18 x 18 in
(45.5 x 45.5 cm)*

tapestry needle(s), size 26

lightweight wadding for mounting (optional)

*1 skein each of stranded cotton in the
following shades:*

		DMC	Anchor
	pale navy	312	979
	deep purple	327	100
	dusty blue	334	977
	medium bronze	732	281
	light bronze	733	280
	pale green-gold	834	874
	dark brown-pink	3721	896

2 skeins of stranded cotton in:

		DMC	Anchor
	green-gold	833	907

*Finished size of design: 10⅛ x 10⅛ in
(25.5 x 25.5 cm)*

becoming a more standard motif in later periods. In conjunction with the purely aesthetic reason, churches were also popular because of the symbolic meanings attached to their different parts. The foundations signify faith, the roof is love, the floor, humility, and the door, obedience. The windows represent hospitality and welcome. The sampler pattern also shows a cross at the top of the steeple as the most powerful Christian symbol and above that sits a weathercock, representing the preacher who, like the weathercock which always turns into the wind, will turn upon the unbeliever and enemies of the church. Altogether a full set of messages from just one motif!

This sampler can be dedicated to either a christening or a marriage. If the shades are too strong for a pastel-based wedding, alter them to reflect the colours of the wedding bouquet. It would also be possible to use sections of the border on bookmarks, or table linen as demonstrated in the following project.

METHOD

Fold the fabric in half lengthwise to find the centre vertical line. Crease lightly. Measure 3 in (7.5 cm) down this line from the top of the fabric and begin stitching at this point following the starting point marked on the chart on page 44.

As with all densely stitched work, I recommend that you tack or oversew the edges to prevent fraying (see page 90) but do this after you have marked the starting stitch, otherwise you will distort the measurements.

Work in cross stitch and back stitch using two strands of cotton over one thread intersection.

From the central starting stitch, work the border either to the left or to the right out to the side, then return to the centre and complete the top line of the border by stitching in the opposite direction. Next work the sides and lastly the bottom line, then stitch the church.

Lastly, personalize your work using the alphabet from the Band Pattern Sampler on page 33 and following the instructions on letter spacing given on page 92.

When the stitching is complete, wash if necessary and press gently from the wrong side (see page 90). Rinse, press and mount using wadding if liked (see page 92).

Napkin

A cross-hatched star design from the large Marriage Sampler (page 43) is used in repeat form for this napkin design. Of course, the shades may be altered to complement those on your china or room decor. The motif could also be used, in single fashion, on a pincushion, card or brooch. Try working the last alternative on fine silk gauze for a delicate effect.

MATERIALS

1 set of Sal-Em dinner napkins in white or cream (see page 93 for stockist)

tapestry needle, size 24

1 skein each of stranded cotton in the following shades:

		DMC	Anchor
	dusty blue	334	977
	light bronze	733	280
	green-gold	833	907

*Finished size of design (single motif):
1 ¾ x 1 ¾ in (4.5 x 4.5 cm)*

METHOD

The motifs are worked in the lower righthand corner of the napkin. Count ten threads up from the fray-stop line of stitching at the bottom of the napkin and ten threads in from the stitching line on the right side. Begin work at this point with a corner stitch from the corner motif shown on the chart on page 44. Work one complete motif, then repeat it on either side leaving two threads between each motif.

Work in cross stitch and back stitch using two strands of cotton over two thread intersections.

When the stitching is complete, rinse if necessary and press the fabric gently from the wrong side.

◆ **A graphic design for enamel work on copper (left) translates into a useful motif shown in the corners of the Marriage Sampler (page 43) and in a group of three to decorate a napkin (above).**

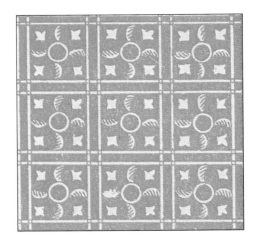

Jane's Lion Sampler

This is a complex sampler for an experienced cross stitcher, which draws on many sources from different decorative and applied arts of the Renaissance. I have included it to serve a similar purpose to that of the traditional spot and band samplers: once worked the piece will be a marvellous reference for motifs and borders as a basis for future projects.

The central motif is Jane Bostocke's lion. It is stitched on her sampler of 1598, shown on page 59. This is the earliest surviving English sampler and can be seen in the Victoria & Albert Museum, London. The lion is a common motif, supporting the idea that samplers provided practice for heraldic embroidery. The pattern forming the central motif of the top border is sourced from the same sampler and this is further exploited on two small projects which follow.

◆ Above: A selection of Renaissance patterns from diverse sources all used to fill different sections of Jane's Lion Sampler.

Right: A small section of the chain worn by this much-adorned 16th century lady makes an interesting linear pattern for the sampler.

Far right: Packed with a wide variety of linear, spot and all-over patterns, this sampler is a source of reference as well as being highly decorative in its own right.

The top righthand corner motif and three of the border patterns are devised from a 1644 sampler worked by 10-year-old Frances Bridon, which also yielded one of the patterns for the Band Pattern Sampler on page 31. How many of today's ten-year-olds could execute such delicate work, I wonder? The remaining three corner motifs and the little design in the middle of the righthand side all come from the treasury of ideas presented by the sampler shown on page 16.

One of the inner border motifs is a small detail taken from jewellery which a lady of the Talbot Family is shown wearing in the picture painted of her. The portrait hangs in the Fitzwilliam Museum, Cambridge and I have included it here to demonstrate the wealth of designs that can be found within paintings.

The remaining motifs come from diverse sources, some of which are illustrated on previous pages. These are:
- A decoration from an illuminated manuscript.
- Tiles from Nilo S. Matteo and the via Luccole in Genoa. Tiles with their bold, graphic designs are a useful source for 'all-over' cover.
- Wood and stone carvings.
- Enamelled copper.
- Pottery decoration.
- A fresco in the central arcade of the Vatican.

METHOD

Fold the fabric in half lengthwise to find the centre vertical line. Crease lightly. Measure 3 in (7.5 cm) down this line from the top of the fabric and begin stitching at this point following the starting point marked on the chart on page 50.

As this is a heavily worked sampler, I recommend that you tack or oversew the edges to prevent fraying (see page 90) after you have established the starting stitch (otherwise the measurements will be incorrect).

Work in cross stitch and back stitch using two strands of cotton over one thread intersection.

Work the sampler in blocks, completing each inner design before extending the internal and external straight lines which form the border for the next design. The temptation will be to work all the straight border lines first but I really would not recommend this, as it is so easy to miscount the number of stitches in a straight line. As the stitched area grows, keep checking your work against the chart to ensure that the pattern blocks are accurately positioned. Alternatively, you may like to commence stitching with the centre lion motif, in which case you should establish the centre of the fabric and match this to the centre stitch on the chart. Once the lion is stitched, continue to work outwards using the same block by block principle as above.

When the stitching is complete, wash if necessary and press gently from the wrong side (see page 90). Rinse, press and mount using wadding is you so wish (see page 92).

MATERIALS

1 piece of white Aida, 16 count, 14 x 14 in (35 x 35 cm)

tapestry needle(s), size 26

lightweight wadding for mounting (optional)

1 skein each of stranded cotton in the following shades:

		DMC	Anchor
	light navy	311	148
	dusty blue	334	977
	medium navy	336	149
	antique pink	316	969
	med. antique pink	3726	970
	dark green	319	217
	light pine green	581	280
	v. pale bright green	954	203
	pale moss green	3348	264
	deep purple	327	100
	pale violet	340	118
	brown green	370	856
	v. pale khaki	472	278
	dark petrol blue	517	170
	light petrol blue	518	168
	pale petrol blue	519	167
	dark sea blue	824	164
	sea blue	826	161
	pale sea blue	827	9159
	v. dark maroon	902	72
	orange-brown	919	340
	new wine	3803	972
	new pink	3806	62
	new dark turquoise	3808	675
	new turquoise	3810	168
	new medium gold	3821	295
	new pale gold	3822	305
	new salmon pink	3824	8
	new dark copper	3829	907

2 skeins of stranded cotton in:

	dk. antique mauve	3740	872

Finished size of design: 7 3/4 x 7 3/4 in (20 x 20 cm)

Cake Band and Decorative Bow

The following seven projects all make use of motifs from the densely stitched sampler on page 49 as a small showing of the huge possibilities for adaptation which this design affords. This delicate design from a 16th century picture in Limoges painted enamel can be used in a multitude of forms, on its own or repeated. I have shown two possible uses here: as a decoration on a cake band and on a bow to hang on the Christmas tree or to include in a Christmas door wreath.

METHOD

To make the cake band, fold the white band in half with short sides together to find the centre vertical line, then count the threads to find the centre of the depth of the Aida. Begin work at this point following the starting stitch on the chart below.

Work in cross stitch and back stitch using two strands of cotton over one thread intersection. Stitch one complete motif, then continue to work motifs along the length of the band in red and green alternately. Repeat the motifs as many times as is necessary to fill the band, leaving enough plain fabric for the hems at each end.

To help protect your work from the icing, a wider ribbon may be placed around the cake underneath the embroidered band.

To make the bow, measure 2 in (5 cm) in from one end of the red band, then calculate the centre point of the depth by counting the number of threads. Start work at this point using the gold metallic thread. Repeat the motifs along the band.

When the stitching is complete, take the two corners of one end of the band placing right sides together and stitch together from the centre fold point to the edges at an angle of 45°. Repeat with the other end. Turn right side out. Press into a point.

Fold the band into a bow shape, crossing the ends but do not tie and leave long tails. Pinch the place where the bow is formed and stitch through all layers of the fabric to hold in place. Take the ribbon and wrap around the pinched place to form a false tie. Stitch into place on the reverse leaving a length of ribbon at one end which is then doubled over and secured with a stitch to form a loop by which to hang the bow.

MATERIALS

1 piece of white Aida band, 2 or 3 in (5 or 7.5 cm) wide, to fit the size of the cake to be decorated

1 piece of red Aida band, 3 in (7.5 cm) wide, 1 yd (1 m) long

tapestry needle, size 24 or 26

1 ribbon, 1 in (2.5 cm) wide, 6 in (15 cm) long in your own choice of colour

red sewing cotton and needle

1 skein each of stranded cotton in the following shades:

		DMC	Anchor
■	*dark green*	319	217
▨	*red*	666	46
▢	*gold metallic*		

Finished size of design (single motif): 1 x 1 in (2.5 x 2.5 cm)

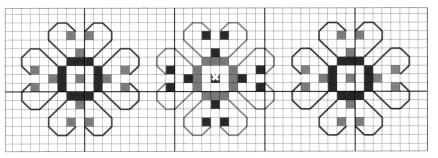

◆ Above: In green and red or simply in gold, this little motif with its origins in a piece of 16th century enamelling, makes a charming band pattern.
Far left: A quickly stitched design to add an individual and personal touch to seasonal decorations.

MATERIALS

*1 piece of cream Aida, 18 count, 6 x 6 in
(15 x 15 cm)*

tapestry needle, size 26

*1 gold pot, 3 in (7.5 cm) in diameter (see
page 93 for stockist)*

*1 piece of iron-on interfacing, same size as
Aida*

*1 skein each of stranded cotton in the
following shades:*

		DMC	Anchor
■	*medium bronze*	732	281
■	*orange-brown*	919	340
■	*petrol blue*	3760	161
▫	*new pale gold*	3822	305

Finished size of design: 2 ³⁄₄ x 2 ³⁄₄ (7 x 7 cm)

◆ **Right: One of the most effective
displays of cross stitch is as an all-
over pattern, as shown in this pot lid
decoration which takes a geometric
design from an Italian church (above)
as its source.**

**Far right: Two variations of a simple
carved wood design embroidered on
pieces to decorate the dining table.**

Venetian Pot

A bas-relief from the church of San Michele in Murano, Venice provides
the inspiration for this project. The motif has been used here in block
repeat form as an embellishment for a pot lid to demonstrate the effect
of overall cover. The design could easily be expanded for a larger project.

METHOD

Fold the fabric in half lengthwise and crosswise to find the centre point.
Crease lightly. Start work at this point following the stitch marked on the
chart below, then expand the design in all directions to cover the area
you wish to decorate.

Work in cross stitch and back stitch using two strands of cotton over
one thread intersection.

When the stitching is complete, wash if necessary and press gently
from the wrong
side (see page
90). Place the
interfacing
centrally on the
reverse of the
work and iron in
position. Trim
and place the fab-
ric centrally in the
pot lid following
the manufactur-
er's instructions.

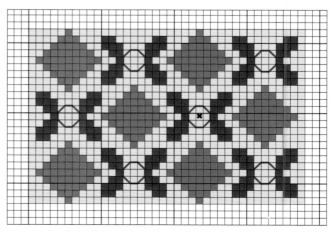

Napkin Holder and Coaster

This project presents a matching set of coaster and napkin holder for the dining table. The set could be extended to include napkins, using the napkin holder band design and working it around the edges. The source for this design is an oak chair back carving shown opposite.

METHOD

To make the napkin holder, fold the band in half lengthwise and crosswise to find the centre point. Crease lightly. Begin work at this point following the starting stitch marked on the relevant chart on page 57.

Work in cross stitch and back stitch using three strands of cotton over one thread intersection.

When the stitching is complete, place the two ends of the band with wrong sides together and stitch a ¼ in (5 mm) seam. Press seam to one side. Turn the circle to the inside and stitch another ¼ in (5 mm) seam to enclose the raw edges. Turn right side out.

To make the coaster: fold the fabric into four to find the centre point. Crease lightly. Begin work at this point following the starting stitch marked on the relevant chart on page 57.

Work in cross stitch and back stitch using three strands of cotton over one thread intersection. Work the circle part of the design first, then 1 in (2.5 cm) of the strip on each side and again at right angles to form a cross shape. Place the interfacing centrally on the reverse of the work and iron in position. Trim to fit the coaster and mount according to the manufacturer's instructions.

MATERIALS

2 pieces of cream or white Aida, 14 count, 13 x 4 in (33 x 10 cm), for the knitting needlecase

1 piece of cream or white Aida, 14 count, 6 x 9 in (15 x 23 cm), for the sewing needlecase

tapestry needle, size 24

2 inner leaves of non-fraying fabric for the sewing needlecase, same size as Aida

2 pieces of lining fabric, 13 x 4 in (33 x 10 cm), for the knitting needlecase

1 piece of lining fabric, 6 x 9 in (15 x 23 cm), for the sewing needlecase

white sewing thread and needle

braid, 24 in (60 cm) long, for knitting needle-case, 20 in (50 cm) for the sewing needlecase

1 skein each of stranded cotton in the following shades:

		DMC	Anchor
	pale pink	605	50
	pale gold	726	295
	gold	783	307
	medium blue	797	132
	pale blue	809	130
	blue-green	991	189
	pale blue-green	993	186
	new wine red	3803	972

Finished size of design (single motif): 2 1/3 x 5/8 in (6 x 1.5 cm)

◆ **Right: Two useful needlecases which make a tidy way of keeping the 'tools of the trade' in order and would make a pretty gift for a stitcher.**

Knitting and Sewing Needlecases

A small decoration on a piece of china (see page 48) provides the inspiration for this floral pattern, which is worked in two variations.

METHOD

To make the knitting needle case, fold one of the pieces of Aida in half with long sides together to find the centre vertical line. Crease lightly. Measure 2 1/2 in (6 cm) down this line from the top of the fabric and start work at this point with the top two starting stitches marked on the chart on page 57 placed on either side of the centre line.

Work in cross stitch and back stitch using two strands of cotton over one thread intersection. Work the motifs down the length of the fabric.

When the stitching is complete, place the two pieces of Aida with right sides together, then position a piece of lining on either side, sandwiching the Aida. Machine stitch or back stitch by hand, using a 1/2 in (1.5 cm) seam allowance, round two long and one short side starting 3/4 in (2 cm) below the top on the first long side. At the top, turn in the sides, then make a hem deep enough to allow the braid to be inserted as a drawstring. Slip stitch in place. Turn to right side.

To make the needlecase, fold the fabric in half with short sides together to find the centre fold. Crease lightly. Now fold the right-hand side of the case in half lengthwise to find the centre vertical line. Use this to place the motifs.

Work in cross stitch and back stitch as above, following the starting stitch marked on the chart on page 57. To make up, see directions on page 70.

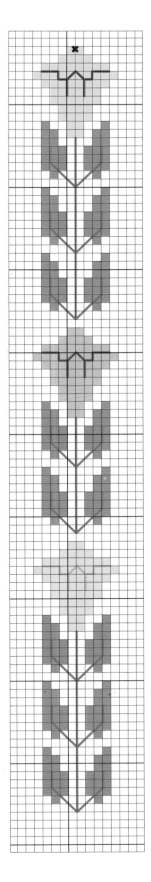

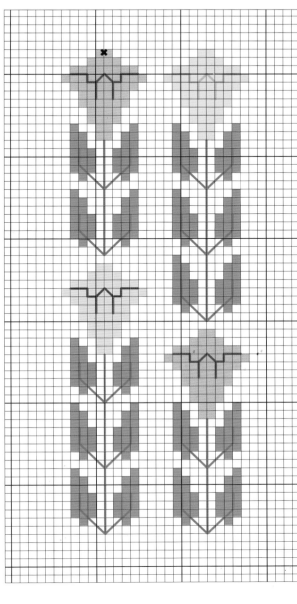

MATERIALS

Napkin Holder and Coaster

1 piece of white Aida band, 2 in (5 cm) wide and 6½ in (17 cm) long for each holder

1 piece of white Aida, 14 count, 5 x 5 in (12.5 x 12.5 cm)

tapestry needle, size 24

white sewing cotton and needle

1 coaster (see page 93 for stockist)

1 piece of iron-on interfacing, same size as 14 count Aida

1 skein each of stranded cotton in the following shades:

		DMC	Anchor
	dark green	319	217
	red	666	46
	dark yellow	444	291

Finished size of design (napkin holder): 4 x 1⅛ in (10 x 3 cm)

Finished size of design (coaster): 2¼ x 2¼ in (5.5 x 5.5 cm)

Far left: Knitting Needlecase
Left: Sewing Needlecase
Below: Napkin Holder and Coaster

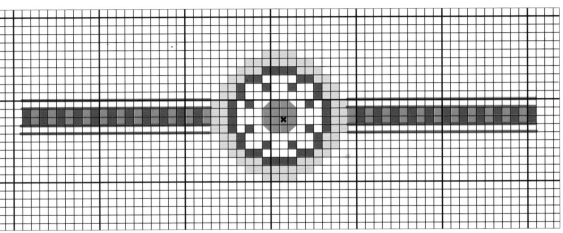

Bookmark, Pot and Card

These three small motifs worked in back stitch and cross stitch, are all derived from Jane Bostocke's famous sampler shown opposite, which also inspired the central motif of the Jane's Lion Sampler (page 49).

The sampler was not rediscovered until 1960 and is the only known dated sampler to have survived from the 16th century. It is a combination of spot and band work and larger than usual for this type of sampler. A variety of stitches, including cross, chain, satin and tent has been used, embellished with seed pearls and black beads.

This sampler is the most marvellous source for design motifs. For these pretty pieces I have adapted a stylized carnation, a grape and vine motif and an acorn pattern; all examples of commonly used motifs of the period. Some of the cottons are used in two of the designs, one skein will suffice for both and all of the pieces only require small amounts.

METHOD

To make the card and the pot, fold the fabric in half lengthwise and crosswise to find the centre point. Crease lightly. Begin work at this point following the starting stitch marked on the relevant chart on page 60.

Work in cross stitch using two strands of cotton and in back stitch using one strand both over one intersection.

When the stitching is complete, press the fabric gently from the wrong side. Place the interfacing centrally on the reverse of the work and iron in position.

Mount the grape design in the pot lid following the manufacturer's instructions and the acorn design in the greetings card blank following the instructions on page 92, using wadding if liked.

To make the bookmark: fold the bookmark into four to find the centre point. Begin work at this point following the starting stitch marked on the relevant chart on page 60. Stitch one complete motif centrally, then repeat the motif above and below the first. Work in cross stitch and back stitch as for the card and pot designs.

◆ **Above: Carrying on a great tradition - motifs from the earliest sampler put to a modern use.**
Far right: This earliest known English sampler, stitched by Jane Bostocke, is crammed with all kinds of intricate patterns, some representational, some geometric, providing a fascinating insight into the decorative work of the late 16th century.

MATERIALS

1 lacy bookmark, for carnation design

1 piece of white Aida, 18 count, 4 x 4 in
(10 x 10 cm), for acorn design

1 piece of white Aida, 14 count, 6 x 6 in
(15 x 15 cm), for grape design

tapestry needle, size 26

2 pieces of iron-on interfacing, same size as
Aida for pot and card

1 pot, 3½ in (9 cm) in diameter, for grape
design (see page 93 for stockist)

1 card mount with 2¼ in (5.5 cm) diameter
aperture, for acorn design (see page 93 for
stockist)

fabric adhesive

lightweight wadding for mounting (optional),
for card

1 skein each of stranded cotton in the
following shades:

		DMC	Anchor
acorn design			
■	black	310	403
■	new green	3818	923
■	new rust	3830	5975
grape design			
■	black	310	403
■	dark royal blue	791	178
■	dark maroon	814	45
■	new green	3818	923
carnation design			
■	medium mauve	208	111
■	green	367	216
■	pale green	368	214
■	dark grey	413	401
■	dark green-gold	832	907

*Finished size of design (single motif,
carnation): 1¾ x 1¾ in (4.5 x 4.5 cm)*

*Finished size of design (grape): 2¾ x 2¾ in
(7 x 7 cm)*

*Finished size of design (acorn): 1¾ x 1¾ in
(4.5 x 4.5 cm)*

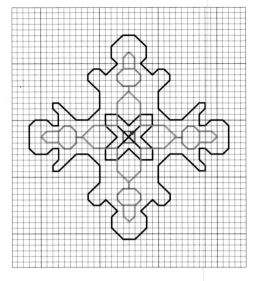

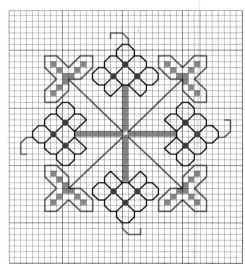

Above: Bookmark

Top right: Card

Right: Pot

Below: Evening Bag

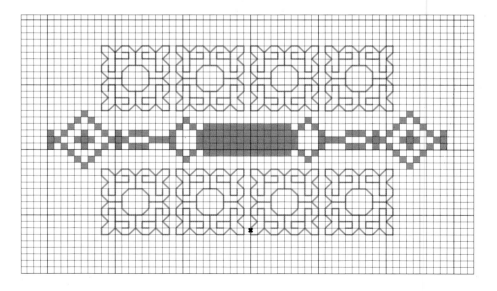

Evening Bag

A repeat pattern originally worked in double running stitch also from the Jane Bostocke sampler of 1598 described on page 58 is used here in silver and gold metallic, thus fulfilling the original aim of sampler work, which was as pattern reference for the embellishment of personal items. The central chequered design is sourced from jewellery adorning the lady in the portrait on page 48, also used on the Jane's Lion Sampler.

I have used a dark blue fabric as the basis for the stitching, you can choose a different colour to match you own outfit but note that the design is more effective when worked on a dark shade of fabric.

METHOD

Fold the Aida in half, with long sides together to find the centre vertical line. Crease lightly. Measure 2 in (5 cm) up this line from the bottom of the fabric and begin stitching at this point following the starting point marked on the relevant chart on page 60. Work in cross stitch and back stitch using two strands of metallic thread over one thread intersection.

When the stitching is complete, press the fabric gently from the wrong side, then lay the piece face up on the work table. Place the lining fabric on top, wrong side up, then the wadding. Machine or hand stitch around three edges using a ½ in (1.5 cm) seam allowance and leaving the unworked, shorter end open. Trim the corners and turn to the right side, enclosing the wadding.

Fold in the raw edges and slip stitch together. Fold the rectangle into three to form a bag shape, with the worked pattern forming the top flap. Oversew the sides forming the pouch, then sew on the braid round the sides of the pouch and the flap.

MATERIALS

1 piece of blue Aida, 18 count, 9 x 14½ in (23 x 37 cm)

1 piece of lining fabric, same size as Aida

1 piece of lightweight wadding, same size as Aida

tapestry needle, size 26

sewing cotton to match fabrics and needle

braid in your choice of colour, 1 yd (1 m) long

1 skein each of metallic threads in the following shades:

▨ gold

▨ silver

Finished size of design: 1⅔ x 3¼ in (4 x 8.5 cm)

◆ **Gold and silver threads make an elegant decoration for an evening accessory.**

Grapevine Commemorative Sampler

A 17th century border design, worked on loosely woven linen mesh, which is to be found in the Embroiderers' Guild collection housed at Hampton Court, forms the basic pattern for this project.

During the 16th and 17th centuries the Italian influence on style was great. Much excavation work of old Roman houses and grounds was undertaken during the Renaissance and many decorative panels embellishing the walls of the houses, caves and grottoes were uncovered. The linear patterns and looped swags were quickly taken up and copied by European designers.

In essence, the style was symmetrical. When mixed with the other popular influences of the time, such as the interlaced Arabic, Turkish and Moorish patterns and the cartouches and scrolls of the ever popular medieval style, the result was rich and flowing.

The linen border used here is a good example of such influences. The designs were often worked in a single colour and, as here, only the background was stitched, leaving the unworked areas to form the pattern. The designs were intended to be used as border embroidery on both personal items, such as collars and cuffs, and on domestic articles, such as bed linen.

The project can be worked as illustrated or for a more complex final effect the border may be worked at the top as well as the bottom of the sampler. The grape and vine design is ambiguous enough to enable the sampler to celebrate a variety of events and the space allowed for the dedication large enough to take a favourite saying or verse.

◆ **Below: A negative image of the popular grapevine design: the background is stitched and the pattern is revealed by the areas of unworked linen.**
Right: Inspired by the 17th century linen border design, this attractive sampler is kept simple by being worked in just three shades.

ALEXANDER
GILBERT

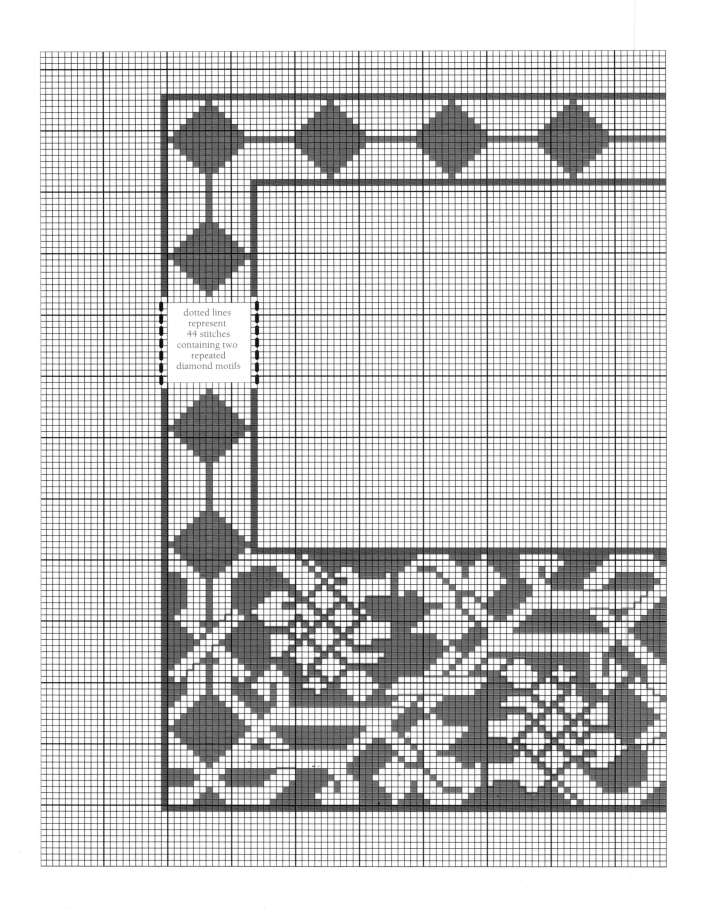

dotted lines
represent
44 stitches
containing two
repeated
diamond motifs

dotted lines
represent
44 stitches
containing two
repeated
diamond motifs

MATERIALS

1 piece of white Aida, 14 count, 18 x 17 in (45.5 x 43 cm)

tapestry needle(s), size 24

lightweight wadding for mounting (optional)

1 skein each of stranded cotton in the following shades:

	DMC	Anchor
dark antique pink	315	896
brown-green	370	856

3 skeins of stranded cotton in:

	DMC	Anchor
sea blue	826	161

Finished size of design: 11½ x 10½ in (29 x 26.5 cm)

METHOD

As with the other large pieces of work, I recommend that you tack or oversew the edges to prevent fraying (see page 90), but do this after you have established the starting stitch, otherwise the measurements will not be accurate.

Measure 3 in (7.5 cm) down from the top right corner of the fabric and 3 in (7.5 cm) in from the righthand side, and begin stitching at this point following the point marked on the chart on page 65.

Work in cross stitch and back stitch using two strands of cotton over one thread intersection.

From the starting stitch, work down the right hand side of the border, then work the deep base border pattern, leaving any back stitch outlining until the main stitching is completed. Now work the left hand side border, checking that the diamonds are exactly aligned with those on the right side, then work the top border.

Lastly, personalize your work either adding a piece of poetry or a dedication to someone special using the alphabet from the Band Pattern Sampler on page 33 and following the instructions on letter spacing given on page 92.

When the stitching is complete, wash if necessary and press gently from the wrong side (see page 90). Rinse, press and mount using wadding if you so wish (see page 92).

Elizabethan Book Cover

A book cover attributed to the Princess Elizabeth, later Elizabeth I of England, and worked when she was 11 years old as a gift for her step-mother Katherine Parr, is the basis for this project. The original was made to cover a volume of 'The Mirroir or Glasse of the Synnefull Soule' and is sewn in gold and silver work on blue corded silk. It has the initials 'K.P.' worked on the centre of each cover.

This project is worked as a panel and edged with braid, to be stitched upon a further piece of fabric which is used to cover the book.

METHOD

Fold the Aida in half, with long sides together to find the centre vertical line. Crease lightly. Measure 2 in (5 cm) down this line from the top of the fabric and begin stitching at this point following the starting point marked on the chart on page 69.

Work the cross stitch using two strands of cotton over one thread intersection. Work the gold back stitch for the central box using one strand over one thread intersection.

Personalize your work with initials charted from the alphabet on page 33 placed centrally within the back-stitched box.

When the stitching is complete, press lightly from the wrong side, then turn under a ½ in (13 mm) hem all round and stitch down. Place the interfacing centrally on the reverse of the work, trim to fit the panel, then iron in place.

This panel can now be attached to a book cover made from contrasting fabric. Wrap the paper around the book you wish to cover and make a pattern, including book flaps.

◆ **Below: The book cover believed to have been worked by Elizabeth I when she was an eleven-year-old princess.**

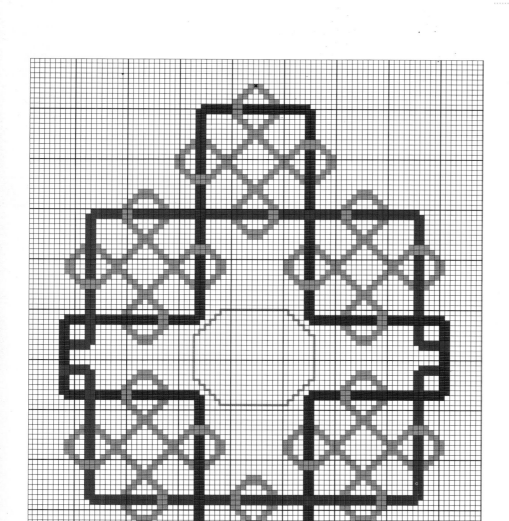

MATERIALS

1 piece of cream Aida, 16 count,
10 ¾ x 8 ¾ in (27 x 22 cm)

1 piece of iron-on interfacing, same size as
the Aida

tapestry needle, size 26

fabric for book cover, e.g. heavy cotton or silk
(see method)

braid (optional)

large piece of scrap paper

1 skein each of stranded cotton in the
following shades:

		DMC	Anchor
■	*dark blue*	796	133
■	*wine red*	816	44
■	*gold metallic*		

Finished size of design: 6 ½ x 4 ⅝ in
(16.5 x 12 cm)

Add ½ in (13 mm) hem allowance to all edges. Cut out the cover fabric to this pattern. Turn under the ½ in (13 mm) hem and stitch down. Place in position round the book and pin the cross-stitched panel to the front of the cover in the desired position. Slip stitch neatly in place and, if you so wish, add braid round the edges. Finally slip stitch the cover flaps to form pockets for the book boards.

◆ **Left: A modern interpretation of the design embroidered by Princess Elizabeth and put to just the same use.**

Italianate Needlecase

The design for this needlecase is derived from an Italian style glazed terracotta cartouche, which forms part of the decoration on the exterior of the Château de Madrid. Medieval in origin, the cartouche continued to be used throughout the Renaissance period in heraldry and architecture, either on its own or to surround emblems and motifs. The motif is used here on its own but it could also be repeated to form a strong border design. Alternatively, the centre part of the design could be omitted and initials placed within the cartouche.

METHOD

Fold the fabric in half with short sides together to find the centre fold line and crease lightly. Now fold the righthand side of the case in half lengthwise and crosswise to find the centre point and crease again. Begin stitching at this point following the starting stitch marked on the relevant chart on page 71.

Work in cross stitch using two strands of cotton over one thread intersection.

When the stitching is complete, press gently from the wrong side and lay face up on the work table. Place the lining fabric on top and machine stitch or back stitch by hand round three sides, leaving a $\frac{1}{2}$ in (1.5 cm) seam allowance. Trim the corners and turn right side out. Turn under the raw edges on the open side and slip stitch to close.

Trim the inner leaves to fit just inside the outer case, then backstitch in position down the centre fold of the case.

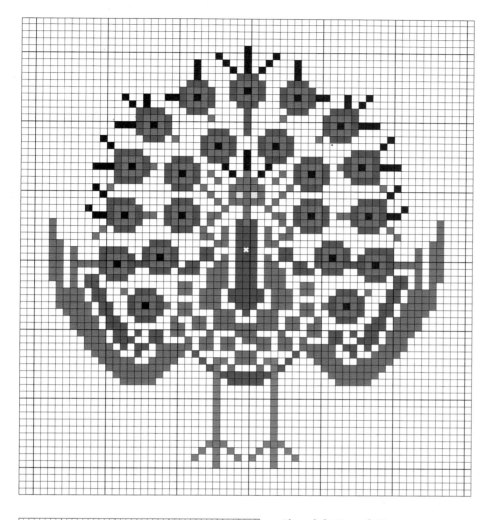

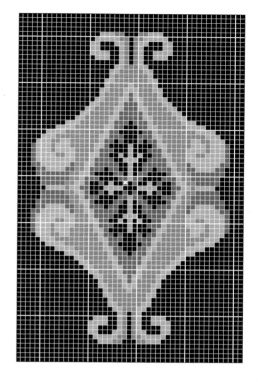

Above left: *Peacock Picture*
Above right: *Italianate Needlecase*
Left: *Spectacles Case*

MATERIALS

*1 piece of black Aida, 18 count, 6 x 9 in
(15 x 23 cm)*

tapestry needle, size 26

1 piece of lining fabric, same size as Aida

*2 inner leaves of non-fraying fabric, same size
as Aida*

black sewing cotton and needle

*1 skein each of stranded cotton in the
following shades:*

		DMC	Anchor
	gold	783	307
	dark dusky pink	3350	65
	dark dusty blue	322	978

*Finished size of design: 3 ¾ x 2 ¼ in
(9.5 x 6 cm)*

◆ Far left (above): The terracotta
cartouche design which has been
translated into a cross stitch motif.
Far left (below): A stylish cartouche in
typical Renaissance style decorates
this little needlecase.

MATERIALS

1 piece of cream Aida, 18 count, 6 x 6 in (15 x 15 cm)

tapestry needle, size 26

1 piece of iron-on interfacing, same size as Aida

1 picture frame, with 3½ in (9 cm) square aperture in mount

lightweight wadding for mounting (optional)

1 skein each of stranded cotton in the following shades:

		DMC	Anchor
	dark cinnamon	433	371
	medium blue	797	132
	new med. turquoise	3809	851
	yellow	743	305
	very dark grey	3799	236

Finished size of design: 3½ x 3 in (8.5 x 7.5 cm)

Peacock Picture

Vinciolo's book of 1587, 'Les Singuliers et Nouveaux Pourtraicts pour Toutes Sortes d'Ouvrages de Lingerie' was an important volume for the English needlewoman, introducing her to the Italian style of cut and lace work. Vinciolo was commissioned by Catherine de Medici to make the extremely large, starched ruffs which she made so popular. He drew upon designs found on Oriental silk fabrics as well as his own original ideas for this work and the results were compiled into his volume for needlewomen to copy. The peacock is taken from one of the black and white charts in his book and presented here in full colour.

METHOD

Fold the fabric in half lengthwise and crosswise to find the centre point. Crease lightly. Begin work at this point following the stitch marked on the chart on page 71.

Work in cross stitch using two strands of cotton over one thread intersection.

When the stitching is complete, press the fabric gently from the wrong side. Trim and mount in the picture frame (see page 92), using wadding in between the embroidery and the backing board if liked.

◆ **The peacock as a symbol of royalty, eternity and luxury, makes a meaningful gift as a picture and would also be a good motif to use on a commemorative sampler.**

Spectacles Case

A beautiful Italian jewelled pendant provides the form for this project, its fluid drop shape used as a single motif on the spectacles case. This is a versatile little design: try using it in single form for greetings cards and stationery sets or as a repeat on towels and table linen. The Renaissance period saw a great usage of jewels and jewellery not only as individual pieces of adornment but also incorporated by the courtly and wealthy into the costumes themselves.

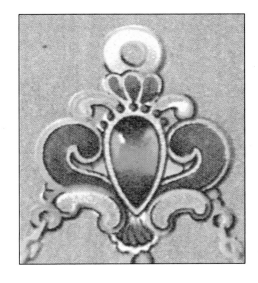

METHOD

Fold one of the pieces of Aida in half lengthwise and crosswise to find the centre point. Crease lightly. Begin work at this point following the stitch marked on the relevant chart on page 71.

Work in cross stitch using two strands of cotton over one thread intersection and in back stitch using one strand for the outlining.

When the stitching is complete, press gently, then place the interfacing centrally on the reverse of the work and iron in position. Repeat to iron on the remaining piece of interfacing to the second piece of Aida.

Pin the fabrics together in the following order: plain Aida, interfacing side up; 1 piece of wadding; 2 pieces of lining; 1 piece of wadding; worked Aida, right side up. Now machine stitch or back stitch by hand leaving a ¼ in (5 mm) seam allowance around the sides and lower edge. Trim across the corners. Turn inside out and repeat the stitching. This will enclose the raw edges. Turn to the right side and fold under the raw edges at the top and slip stitch to close. Finally, slip stitch the braid round all the edges.

MATERIALS

2 pieces of white Aida, 16 count, each 8 x 5 in (20 x 12.5 cm)

2 pieces of wadding, lining and iron-on interfacing, all same size as Aida

tapestry needle, size 26

braid, 28 in (71 cm) long

sewing cotton in white and in the chosen colour of your braid

1 skein each of stranded cotton in the following shades:

		DMC	Anchor
	pale silver	762	23
	dark green-gold	832	907
	new wine red	3803	972
	new pink	3806	62
	new blue	3807	122
	new green	3818	923
	new gold	3820	306
outline			
	pale silver	as above	
	pale grey	318	399

Finished size of design: 2¼ x 3⅛ in (6 x 8 cm)

◆ **Above left: A pretty decoration for a practical spectacles case.**
Above: A design for a jewelled pendant reminiscent of the one in the painting on page 48.

Towel

Birds and fish feature strongly on spot or random samplers at this time and often in the form of 'slips'. Random motifs would be worked using coloured silks in tent stitch on linen canvas. These motifs would then be cut out and appliquéd onto domestic items, such as bed covers and drapes. One such sampler provides the motif for this towel design. Often highly coloured, the motifs may well have been sourced from the popular printed woodcut pattern books of the time.

METHOD

Pin, then tack the waste canvas to the righthand lower corner of the towel (see page 89). Measure 2 in (5 cm) in from the righthand side and 3 ½ in (9 cm) up from the lower edge of the towel. Start work at this point following the starting stitch marked on the chart opposite.

Work in cross stitch using three stands of cotton over one intersection of the canvas.

When the stitching is complete, use tweezers to withdraw the warp and weft of the waste fabric, leaving just the design in place.

◆ **Below: The fish taken from the embroidery opposite makes an appropriate motif for a towel.**

MATERIALS

1 towel, white or pastel shade
darning needle
waste canvas, 14 count, 9 x 9 in (23 x 23 cm)
1 skein each of stranded cotton in the
following shades:

		DMC	Anchor
	dark brick red	347	13
	pale brick red	760	9
	palest brick red	3713	968
	dark grey	413	401
	dark khaki	469	267
	pale khaki	471	265
	light sea blue	813	160
	dark sea blue	824	164

Finished size of design: 4 ³/₄ x 4 in
(12 x 10 cm)

◆ Random motifs of birds, insects and
fish stitched in the early 17th century.

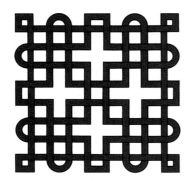

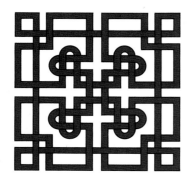

MATERIALS

2 pieces of Aida, one blue, one white, 18 count, each 4 x 4 in (10 x 10 cm)

tapestry needle, size 26

2 pieces of iron-on interfacing, same size as Aida

1 gold pot with 2 ½ in or 3 in (6 or 7.5 cm) diameter lid (see page 93 for stockist)

1 card blank with 2 ½ in (6 cm) aperture

lightweight wadding for mounting in card (optional)

1 skein each of stranded cotton in the following shades:

		DMC	Anchor
☐	white	blanc	1
▨	wine red	816	44

Finished size of design: 1 ¼ x 1 ¼ in (3 x 3 cm)

◆ **Above: Two knot garden plans from a late 16th century book of designs. Right: The abstract designs shown in two different but equally successful mounts: on a greetings card and a pot lid.**

Pot and Card

Two little designs based upon knot garden plans from 'The Gardener's Labyrinth' of 1577 written by Thomas Hill. The Renaissance period saw a great flowering of interest in gardens and gardening and no grand or merchant's house was complete unless it contained at least one knot garden within its grounds.

Often laid out in germander, hyssop, fragrant thyme or lavender, the greater the intricacy, the more greatly they were admired. Many gardening manuals were compiled at this time and many featured woodcut prints of complex knot designs for gardeners to copy. To add definition coal dust, powdered brick or sweet smelling flowers or herbs were often laid between the knots.

METHOD

Work as follows for both pieces.

Fold the fabric in half lengthwise and crosswise to find the centre point. Crease lightly. Begin work at this point following the starting stitch marked on the relevant chart on page 77.

Work in back stitch using two strands of cotton over one thread intersection.

When the stitching is complete, press the fabric gently from the wrong side. Place the interfacing centrally on the reverse of the work and iron in position. Mount the design in the pot lid following the manufacturer's instructions and the card design following the instructions on page 92.

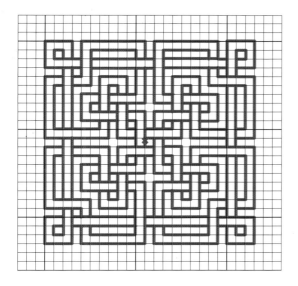

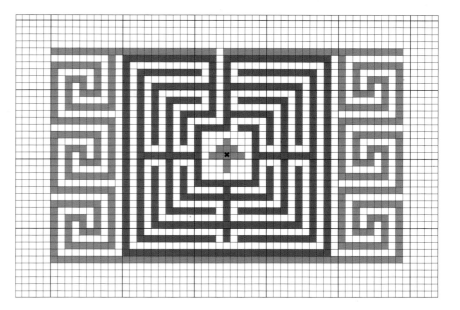

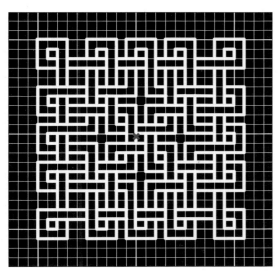

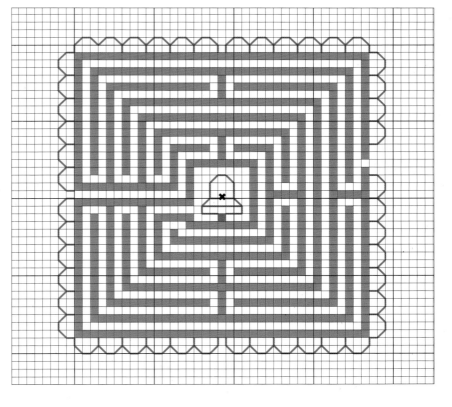

Top left: Pot
Middle left: Card
Bottom left: 16th century maze design
Top right: Calendar, first design
Bottom right: Calendar, second design

MATERIALS

*1 piece of white Aida, 14 count, 8 x 7 in
(20 x 18 cm)*

*1 piece of white Aida, 14 count, 7½ x 9 ½ in
(19 x 24 cm)*

tapestry needle, size 24

2 calendar blocks

ribbon, 6 in (15 cm) long, 1 in (2.5 cm) wide

stiff card, 6 x 4½ in (15 x 11.5 cm)

fabric adhesive

1 pair of bell pull ends, 6 in (15 cm) in width

*1 skein each of stranded cotton in the
following shades:*

		DMC	Anchor
first design			
■	*v. dark khaki*	937	268
▨	*new brown*	3826	349
second design			
▨	*orange-brown*	919	340
■	*v. dark khaki*	937	268

*Finished size of first design: 3½ x 2¼ in
(9 x 5.5 cm)*

*Finished size of second design: 3 x 3 in
(7.5 x 7.5 cm)*

◆ **Above: Maze design from the mid 16th
century.**
**Right: Have fun working out the path
through the maze as you stitch these
two calendar mounts.**

Calendars

Two designs for Renaissance mazes by Serlio (1566) feature here to be
mounted as calendar holders. Mazes were an extension of and in
principle similar to the knot gardens. They were planted in the grounds
of large houses and were as much a source of fun as those grown today.

METHOD

To make the first design, fold the fabric in half lengthwise and crosswise
to find the centre point. Crease lightly. Begin work at this point following
the starting stitch marked on the relevant chart on page 77. Work in
cross stitch using three strands of cotton over one thread intersection.

When the stitching is complete, place the fabric centrally over the stiff
card, right side up. Trim across the corners to within ⅛ in (3 mm) of the
card, then turn the edges over and secure to the back of the card with
fabric adhesive. Cut the ribbon in half. Fold one piece to make a loop
and glue to the top of the card. Glue the other piece of ribbon to the
lower edge of the card and glue the calendar block in the middle. Hem
the end of the ribbon to prevent fraying if necessary.

To make the second design, fold the fabric in half lengthwise to
find the centre vertical line. Measure 3½ in (9 cm) down this line and
commence stitching with the top centre marked stitch on the chart. Work
in cross stitch as above and in back stitch using one strand of cotton.

When the stitching is complete, turn under and stitch a ½ in
(1.5 cm) hem on the long sides. At the top and bottom ends insert
the bell pull ends and turn under a hem of ¾ in (2 cm). Glue the
calendar block beneath the worked design.

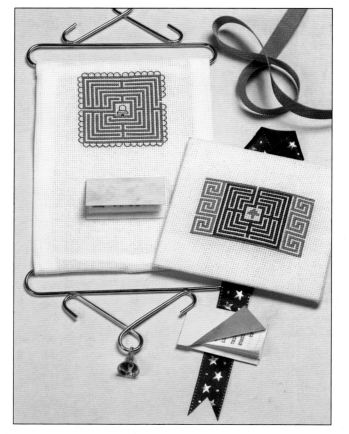

Fleur de Lys Pincushion

The twist border for this pincushion is based on a design painted on pottery from the Gubbio district in Italy. Similar twisted motifs are commonly found in many of the applied and decorative arts throughout the Renaissance period. Complementary to the twist, the stylized fleur de lys diaper pattern, originally adapted from the lily flower, has a royal representation as the heraldic lily of France.

METHOD

Fold the fabric in half lengthwise and crosswise to find the centre point. Crease lightly. Begin work at this point following the starting stitch marked on the chart on page 80.

Work in cross stitch using two strands of cotton over one thread intersection and in back stitch using one strand over one intersection.

When the stitching is complete, press gently from the wrong side. Place the two pieces of Aida right sides together and machine stitch or back stitch by hand round three sides, leaving a ½ in (1.5 cm) seam allowance. Trim the corners, then turn right side out. Fill the cushion with the stuffing to the desired density, then turn under the seam allowance on the open side and slip stitch to close. Decorate as desired.

◆ **Above: Louis XI of France shown robed in the heraldic lily in an illustration from a 16th century French manuscript.**
Left: The ubiquitous fleur de lys motif is nicely framed by a twisted border and well displayed on this pincushion.

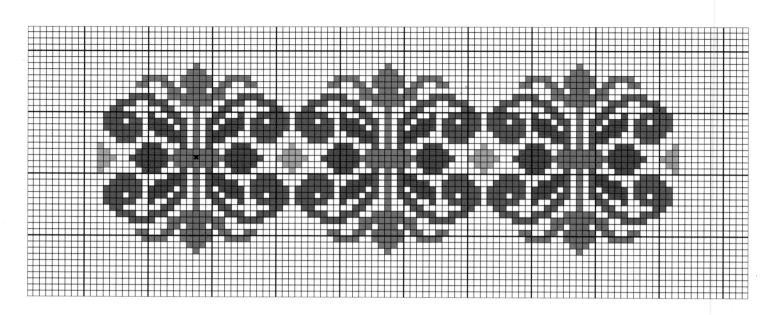

MATERIALS

Fleur de lys Pincushion

2 pieces of white Aida, 18 count, 5 x 5 in (12.5 x 12.5 cm)

tapestry needle, size 26

polyester stuffing

white sewing cotton and needle

braid or tassels

1 skein each of stranded cotton in the following shades:

		DMC	Anchor
	pale navy	312	979
	dark antique pink	315	896
	pale green-gold	834	874
	pale dusty blue	3325	129

Finished size of design: 3 ¼ x 3 ¼ in (8 x 8 cm)

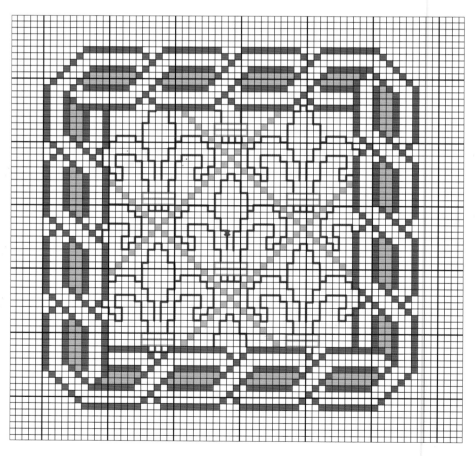

Top: Ornamental Band
Right: Fleur de lys Pincushion

Ornamental Band

The design of this piece is based upon a French ornamental frieze pattern. The shape, which occurs quite frequently in Renaissance architectural design, lends itself very well to a repeat pattern.

METHOD

Fold fabric in half with short sides together to find the centre vertical line. Count up the threads to find the centre point on this line.

Commence stitching at this point following the centre marked square on the chart on page 80. Work in cross stitch using three strands of cotton over one thread intersection. Stitch one complete motif, then continue adding motifs on either side until the desired length of band is filled.

MATERIALS

1 piece of white Aida band, 3 in (7.5 cm) wide, to length required

tapestry needle, size 24

1 skein each of stranded cotton in the following shades:

		DMC	Anchor
	deep purple	327	100
	dark petrol blue	517	170
	gold	783	307
	orange-brown	919	340

Finished size of design (single motif): 2 x 2 in (5 x 5 cm)

◆ **Opposite and below: This typical frieze design makes an obvious linear pattern for a band decoration.**

MATERIALS

2 pieces of white Aida, 14 count, 14 x 14 in (35 x 35 cm) or

1 piece Aida and 1 piece of backing fabric of your own choice

tapestry needle, size 24

1 cushion pad, 12 in (30 cm) square

braid, 1¾ yds (1.75 m)

1 skein each of stranded cotton in the following shades:

		DMC	Anchor
■	*purple*	552	99
■	*new med. turquoise*	3809	851
■	*medium sea blue*	825	162
■	*new wine red*	3803	972
■	*dark green-gold*	832	907

Finished size of design: 9¼ x 9¼ in (23.5 x 23.5 cm)

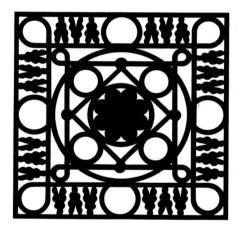

◆ **Right: A simple but effective pattern for a cushion inspired by a garden design from the end of the 15th century (above).**

Box Hedge Cushion

Colonna's box hedge design as sourced from his book, 'Hypherotomachia', provides the shape and form for this simple cushion pattern. Colonna's book of 1499 is housed at the British Museum in London. The outer border is also used as the framework for the more complex piece, Jane's Lion Sampler on page 49.

METHOD

First tack or oversew the edges of the fabric to prevent fraying (see page 90), then fold the Aida in half lengthwise and crosswise to find the centre point. Crease lightly. Start work seven holes to the right of this point following the stitch marked on the chart on page 83.

Work in cross stitch using three strands of cotton over one thread intersection to give a denser look to the stitching.

When the stitching is complete, remove tacking and press gently from the wrong side. Make up the cushion following the instructions given for the cushion cover on page 29.

Chart-only samplers

The following pages feature two pieces of original source material linked to fully charted adaptations for you to incorporate into your own sampler designs. They both present textiles from the Renaissance period and are marvellous examples of the intricacy of design and standard of embroidery of the time.

These pieces can be stitched by following the charts exactly and will make stunning pictures in their own right. Alternatively, they can be adapted to your own requirements or split up and used as a motif library. Details on how to estimate the size of fabric required are given on page 92.

PAGES 85 TO 86

CHERRY TREE SAMPLER

This photograph shows part of an English cushion cover embroidered in the last quarter of the sixteenth century. It is worked in silk and silver thread and depicts a hunting and hawking scene, the pictorial elements of which are charmingly arranged symmetrically about the central tree rather than as a straightforward narrative scene. Animals are a popular motif in Renaissance embroidery, sometimes they are products of the stitcher's imagination, sometimes, as here, they are lifelike representations.

The piece could be made into a commemorative sampler by embroidering names in place of the little flowers at the base of the tree. You could surround the tree with one of the borders from the other large sampler projects in the book or you could make up a border from either one or both of the little flowers. Alternate the two flowers or use one flower reversing it every other repeat.

PAGES 87 TO 88

ELISABETH'S BAND SAMPLER

This photograph shows a detail from the lower half of a sampler stitched in 1629 and just signed 'Elisabeth'. The whole piece is now kept in the Fitzwilliam Museum, Cambridge. It is 26 $\frac{1}{2}$ in (67 cm) long and contains a wonderful selection of band patterns which would probably have been used as reference for embroidery to be carried out on the borders of household linen, such as on the handkerchief in the photograph on page 13. Floral motifs were the most common and were ingeniously incorporated into geometric designs.

The patterns on page 88 which have been charted from this sampler could be put to the same use. You could stitch them as borders on towels, tablecloths, napkins or even on small curtains.

Alternatively, stitch the chart as it is, add your name at the base and turn it into a wallhanging following the directions on page 34.

Practical Details

FABRICS

Cross stitch is mostly worked on evenweave fabrics - those which have a well-defined, equal warp (vertical) and weft (horizontal) thread, woven in such a way that there are the same number of warp as of weft threads in any square of fabric. Evenweave fabric comes in a variety of types and sizes, which are graded according to the number of threads or holes per inch with the highest number denoting the finest weave and consequently producing the finest stitch. This grading of fabric is referred to as the 'count' of the fabric, so that 18 count fabric will have 18 holes and threads to the inch (2.5 centimetres). Grades range from 10 count through to 26. If a novice, I suggest you start with projects on a lower count (14, for example) and when you are conversant with the basic skill move to the finer or higher counts.

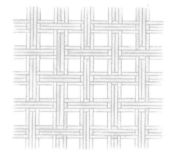

Aida is a widely available type of evenweave fabric and many of the projects in this book are worked on it in various counts. It is woven with groups of warp and weft threads bulked together and woven as one unit, which leaves clearly defined holes between and makes it easy to see where to place the stitches.

Hardanger, a type of evenweave in which pairs of threads are woven together, is also available and the same principles apply.

Lugana is another type of evenweave. A 25 count is available in a variety of shades and is a lovely fabric for bellpulls and wall hangings, as it is softer than Aida but weightier, so that it hangs well. It also has the advantage that, like linens, it can be worked over one or two threads.

Also featured in this book are products made from 'Sal-Em' fabric, an American-produced fabric, cut to the shape of napkins or traycloths with frayed edges and a pre-stitched line around the edges to prevent further fraying. It can be used either for fine stitches worked over one thread to form 26 count or over two threads to form 13 count. If unavailable, a 26 count linen could be used. You could, then, either hem or fray the edges yourself.

Linen is also suitable. This is a plain-weave, i.e. a fabric in which a single weft is woven alternately over and under a

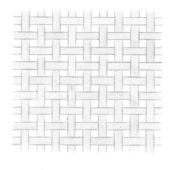

single warp, but is still suitable for cross-stitch work as the weaving of the warp and weft threads is equally spaced throughout the fabric.

Special silk fabric is also used, this has a very high count and needs to be stretched into a frame, to make it manageable for stitching. It is available in pre-stretched form (see page 93) and is supplied with a fine needle. Make sure you are working in a good, bright light when stitching silk, as it is very fine work.

All the fabrics come in a variety of shades and colours. I have used mostly cream and white in this series, but do try experimenting with other shades. Maybe your specialist needlecraft store has a few remnant pieces you could try at not too high a cost for experimentation.

Waste canvas

Other fabrics can be used if your eye and patience are good, but do not attempt to use these until you have mastered the craft.

Waste canvas, available from specialist stores can help with the stitching of non-defined fabric, that is fabric which does not have an obvious grid of threads to work over, such as towelling or velvet. Waste canvas provides a temporary grid, which can be removed after it has been stitched over.

Pin or tack a piece of waste canvas 1 in (2.5 cm) larger all round than the design to be stitched onto the fabric you wish to embroider. Work your stitches over it but be careful not to pull up the stitches too tightly. Once the stitching is

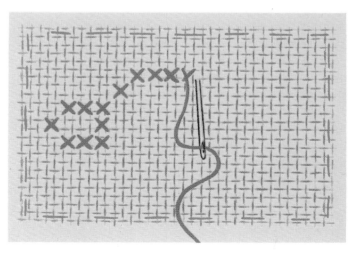

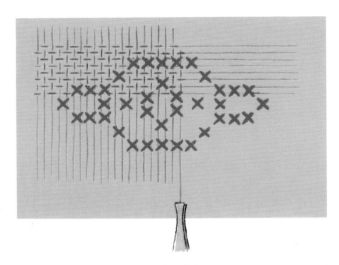

completed, draw out the threads of the waste canvas one by one with tweezers. They should release quite easily as long as your tension has not been too severe!

Care of fabric

All the evenweaves and linen launder beautifully and the stranded cottons used throughout the books are colourfast. If you are in any doubt about whether your threads are colourfast, do a test wash using a little of all the colours on a small piece first. When you have completed your project, if you feel it has become slightly grubby from handling, just wash gently in warm, soapy water, then rinse, to revitalise it. You will also be able to re-stiffen the evenweave Aida by doing this, which will make it easier to mount, as it does tend to soften while being worked. Roll up the embroidery in a dry towel to take out excess moisture, then leave the work on a flat surface to dry naturally. When dry, gently press the embroidery from the wrong side on a dry towel base with a medium-hot steam iron. The fabric can also be given a gentle press in this way during the stitching of a large project, if you feel it has become too limp.

THREADS

Every shade imaginable can be purchased! Half the fun is deciding which to use. Metallic threads are also popular and can add quite a sparkle to your work but the mainstay thread for cross stitch is stranded cotton. It is so-called because each thread is made up of six strands, which are separated to work with, the number of strands altering dependent on the count of the fabric.

As a rough guide on 10 to 14 count use three strands (unless the design is so dense you prefer to use two strands on 14); on 16 to 22 use two strands and on higher counts, one strand.

Other threads, such as crochet cotton, Danish flower threads, coton à broder and stranded silk are also suitable for cross stitch, though the thicker single strand threads should only be used on low counts of fabric.

Use of threads

As suggested, use different numbers of strands for different counts of fabric but universally do not thread your needle with more than a 14 in (35 cm) length at any time. A longer thread will eventually fray in the needle as it is drawn repeatedly through the fabric and leave a feathery thread on the stitching; it may, indeed, even fray out and break.

NEEDLES

Always use blunt-ended tapestry needles. The general rule regarding size is that the eye of the needle should be able to pass through the fabric without distorting the weave and leaving a larger hole. Size 24 is perfect for counts up to 14 and size 26 is fine for other higher counts; on silk use an even finer needle - size 28 or higher - as these are often up to 48 count!

FRAMES

Hoop frames are often used to prevent distortion of the fabric caused by an over-tight tension. Try a small one if you wish, your needlecraft shop will advise you and let you handle the various sizes to see which is comfortable for you. Personally, I only use one when working with floppy fabrics to help keep my tension even. I find generally I like to be able to manoeuvre the fabric in my hands without the constraint of the hoop, the natural stiffness of some fabrics being enough to keep tension balanced. So, whether or not to use a frame is very much your choice.

SETTING TO WORK

Before starting fix a short piece of each thread to a strip of card and number it. This will help you identify the shade, invaluable if you find yourself working in a poor light (which should be avoided) or artificial light when tones, particularly of blues, greens and pinks can subtly alter.

With larger projects it is best (time consuming, I know) to protect the edges of the fabric to prevent fraying, which linen, in particular, is prone to do. To do this, either turn under a small hem all round and tack down or bind the edges with masking tape. This is generally unnecessary with small projects.

The starting point on a stitching chart is generally indicated, as is the case for all the projects in these books. For small designs this is usually in the centre, so that it is helpful to be able to find the centre of your fabric quickly. To do this fold the fabric in half lengthwise and crosswise and crease lightly. For larger projects you may find it useful to tack through the centre vertical and horizontal lines created by folding the fabric, so that these provide permanent reference points when stitching the design. On smaller projects just the creased cross should be enough to get you started. Some patterns give the start stitch in one corner or in the middle of one edge of the pattern, so you will not need to do the above tacking or creasing, just follow the instructions as to the start point.

Thread your needle with the directed number of strands. Do not knot the end as this creates lumps which make an uneven surface on the embroidery and knots can unravel. To commence the first stitch, pull the thread through from the reverse side leaving a tail of about 2 inches (5 cm).

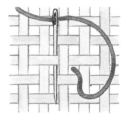

◆ **Single cross stitch**

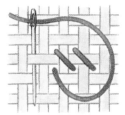

◆ **Cross stitch row**

Hold this tail under the fabric as you work the next stitch. After a few stitches you can either darn the tail in at the back or catch it under with the subsequent stitches. Fasten off by drawing the thread, on the reverse side, through the back of some stitches.

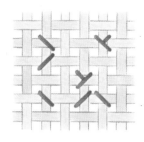

◆ **Half cross stitch**

All the projects in this book use simple cross stitch for most of the design, half cross stitch for some of the shaping and back stitch for outlining. Use the simple half cross stitch for shaping on the edge of a motif and the three quarters version when required in the middle of a design.

If you are a novice, follow the diagrams on a spare piece of fabric to practise.

It is important that the top half of the stitches should all slant in the same direction, otherwise the finished work will look uneven.

All the patterns are worked from colour charts. One square on the chart represents one stitch worked over one or two thread inter- sections on the fabric as directed in the individual instructions. Half squares on the chart denote half cross

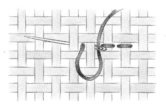

◆ **Backstitch**

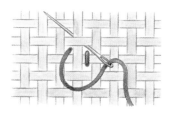

◆ **Angled backstitch**

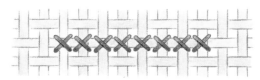

◆ **Over one thread intersection**

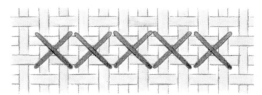

◆ **Over two thread intersections**

stitches, the direction of the diagonal indicating the direc- tion of the stitch. If stitches of one shade are scattered close by each other but not immediately abutting each other, it is acceptable to thread the strands through the backs of some of the other stitches to the next point of stitching, but do this only where there is close proximity of stitch, otherwise the overall tension will become distorted.

Using more than one needle

It is useful, when working a design where groups of stitches in the same shade are close to each other, to use more than one needle. When you have stitched the first group, take the needle through to the reverse of the fabric and secure it loosely in a position where it will not interfere with the next stitches you will work. Using the second needle, work the second shade and fasten the needle at the back of the work, as before. Now remove the first needle and thread it through the back of the stitches just worked, so that it is in the right position to work the second group of stitches in the first shade. This can only be done where groups of stitches in the same shade are separated by just three or four squares. If you carry thread over a larger distance, you may produce an uneven tension and on a low count of fabric the lines of thread may show through to the front.

It is also helpful to have several needles threaded with different shades at the start of a complicated project. This saves time once you are stitching.

Estimating fabric size

The finished size of the stitching area is given with each project, so that if you wish to adapt the design you can work out how the dimensions will change.

If you wish to work one of the projects in this book on a different count of fabric from that recommended, you will need to calculate how much fabric to allow, which is very simple. Count the number of squares on the design chart a) down one vertical edge and b) across one horizontal edge. Divide each of these figures by the count of the fabric you wish to use, e.g. by 14 or 16. This will give you the finished design in inches. Multiply by 2.54 if you wish to have the size in centimetres.

If the work is to be mounted in a frame, add 6 in (15 cm) to each dimension for the fabric size. This allows a good 3 in (7.5 cm) for the framer to use and a 1 in (2.5 cm) hem allowance (to prevent fraying while working).

For fabric size on smaller projects, add 3 in (7.5 cm) to the dimensions of the design, and to fit a particular mount, measure its width and depth, then add on 3 in (7.5 cm).

Letter spacing

This is best worked out on graph paper first, to give a good visual image of how the letters will look. Map out the letters in each horizontal row in pencil on the graph paper, leaving one stitch square between each letter and three between each word. Note that letters which have sloping sides, such as A, W, V, may look better more closely grouped, i.e. without the unstitched square in between.

Now count up the number of horizontal squares in the row and divide by two to find the central point. Where the letters are to be placed centrally on the design, this point will correspond to the centre vertical line of the design. Begin stitching at this point.

For designs where the text is positioned off-centre, refer to the appropriate chart for the starting point. Do map out the letters on graph paper first, though, as you may need to adjust the placing slightly.

FINISHING OFF AND MOUNTING

Tidy your work as you stitch, fastening each thread off by darning it into the back other stitches. Snip off any loose ends.

If the piece needs to be cleaned or freshened up, follow the instructions for washing and pressing given above.

Mounting into card-based mounts, e.g. calendars, greeting cards

Trim the finished piece of work to a slightly smaller size than the mount. Touch fabric adhesive to the edges of the mount and with the design uppermost on a flat surface, place the mount, centrally or as directed, onto the design. At this stage you can pad the design with a little wadding to bring it forward in the mount and soften the edges of the cut-out area. To do this, cut a piece of lightweight wadding just a little larger than the aperture of the mount, touch with glue and fix to the reverse of the embroidered piece. Next glue around the edges of the back of the card or mount backing board and attach it to the back of the embroidery, enclosing the design. Take your time, I have seen too many examples of beautiful stitchwork ruined by bad mounting.

Pots and jars

Back your work with iron-on interfacing before placing in the mount. This has a dual purpose a) it will help prevent fraying and b) it will enable the design to sit more firmly in the mount and not crumple. Iron the interfacing on before you trim the fabric to size. Follow the manufacturers' instructions to assemble the mounts, which are usually simply a matter of trimming the embroidery to fit and placing it in the jar or pot with the backing material in a particular sequence.

Pictures

It is well worth paying for professional mounting. All the effort you have put into the stitching deserves the best!

I like to stretch my work over lightweight wadding as I think it gives a good relief, softening the lines and pushing the stitching forward. A professional framer will lace the work with the wadding over the backing board for you.

A FINAL WORD

Do keep your work in a bag in between stitching: the fabric does tend to pick up dust. But most importantly, after all the rules of 'do's and don'ts', enjoy your craft, be experimental and have fun with creating and stitching the heirlooms of the future!

ACKNOWLEDGEMENTS

The Author and Publishers would like to thank the following people for their help in the production of this book:

For supplying props for photography: Past Times, Witney , Oxon, OX8 6BH, UK

For suppying materials for the projects:

DMC Creative World, Pullman Road, Wigston, Leicestershire, LE18 2DY, UK

Impress, Slough Farm, Westhall, Halesworth, Suffolk IP19 8RN, UK

Framecraft Miniatures Ltd, 372-376 Summer Lane, Hockley , Birmingham, B19 3QA, UK (with stockists worldwide)

Impress, Slough Farm, Westhall, Halesworth, Suffolk IP19 8RN, UK

For help with the stitching:

Lynn Blackledge, Sally Harvey, Sally Mason, Barbara Matthews, Gwen Reah and Gillian South

STOCKISTS

Teapot stand; dressing table set; Sal-Em products; pots; lacy bookmark; coaster: Framecraft Miniatures Ltd

Greetings cards; gift tags: Impress

KITS

All the stitched projects within this book may be purchased in kit form (excluding charts) from:

Stitchkits, 8 Danescourt Road, Tettenhall, Wolverhampton, WV6 9BG, UK

PHOTOGRAPH CREDITS

p. 10, p. 13, p. 85 E T Archive; p. 14 Derek E. Witty, Goodhurst Collection; p. 16, p. 17, p. 59, p. 75 Courtesy of the Trustees, Victoria and Albert Museum/ (photographer); p.23, p. 30, p. 42, p. 46, p. 48 ,p. 53, p. 54, p. 55 from 'The Grammar of Ornament', Studio Editions, 1986; p.30, p. 48, p. 73 from 'Renaissance Ornament, Wordsworth Editions, 1991; p. 70, p. 81 from 'The Encyclopedia of Ornament', Studio Editions, 1988; p. 34, p. 48, p. 87 Fitzwilliam Museum, Cambridge; cover and p. 40 The National Trust Photographic Library/Hawkley Studios; p. 42 Zaanland Museum of Antiquities; p. 62 The Embroiderers' Guild Dudley Moss; p. 67 Bodleian Library Oxford, MS Cherry 36, cover; p. 79 Bibliotheque Nationale, Paris/Bridgeman Art Library